# Brazil Inside Out

'From football to the Amazon forest, *Brazil Inside Out* smoothly surveys the vast landscape of Brazilian society, economics and politics. Longtime Brazil hands Jan Rocha and Francis McDonagh share their expert knowledge in a compact and readable volume, perfect for the long flight down to the World Cup – and a second reading on the way home.'
*Linda Rabben is an American anthropologist, human rights advocate and author of books about Brazilian and other human rights issues.*

'*Brazil Inside Out* is a great short read for those who want to learn about this huge, fascinating, complex and contradictory nation, written with real insight into what makes Brazil and Brazilians tick.
*Liz Throssell is a former BBC correspondent in Brazil*

'Whether you are a regular traveller to Brazil or visiting for the first time, *Brazil Inside Out* guarantees to entertain as well as to inform. Rocha and McDonagh are both expert insiders, but they wear their knowledge lightly. The result is one of the most insightful, enjoyable introductions to Brazil for quite some time.'
*Oliver Balch is author of* Viva South America!

'Latin America Bureau are past masters at providing informative and insightful introductions to the region. With this guide they've combined regional knowledge with football insight to produce the indispensable read for World Cup 2014, home and away.'
*Mark Perryman is author of* Ingerland: Travels with a Football Nation

---

## Latin America Bureau (LAB)

LAB is an independent charitable organisation, based in London, which provides news, analysis and information on Latin America, reporting consistently from the perspective of the region's poor, oppressed or marginalized communities and social movements. LAB brings an alternative, critical awareness and understanding of Latin America to readers throughout the English-speaking world.

LAB is widely known for its books and operates a website, updated daily, in which it carries news and analysis on Latin America and reports from our partners and correspondents in the region (www.lab.org.uk).

# Brazil Inside Out

## People, Politics and Culture

Jan Rocha and Francis McDonagh

PRACTICAL ACTION
Publishing

Practical Action Publishing Ltd
The Schumacher Centre
Bourton on Dunsmore, Rugby,
Warwickshire CV23 9QZ, UK
www.practicalactionpublishing.org

ISBN 978-1-85339-847-6 Hardback
ISBN 978-1-85339-848-3 Paperback
ISBN 978-1-78044-847-3 Library Ebook
ISBN 978-1-78044-848-0 Ebook

Rocha, Jan and McDonagh, Francis (2014) Brazil Inside Out:
People, Politics and Culture, Rugby, UK: Practical Action Publishing
<http://dx.doi.org/9781780448473.000>.

Since 1974, Practical Action Publishing has published and disseminated
books and information in support of international development work
throughout the world. Practical Action Publishing is a trading name
of Practical Action Publishing Ltd (Company Reg. No. 1159018), the
wholly owned publishing company of Practical Action. Practical Action
Publishing trades only in support of its parent charity objectives and
any profits are covenanted back to Practical Action
(Charity Reg. No. 247257, Group VAT Registration No. 880 9924 76).

Edited by Sue Branford
Sub-edited by Ralph Smith
Picture editing by Ali Rocha
Front cover photograph by © lazyllama/fotolia.com
Back cover photographs (from top to bottom) © Ali Rocha,
Douglas Engle, Julio Etchart, and Christian Tragni
Cover design by Baseline Arts, Oxford
Typeset by Bookcraft Ltd, Stroud, Gloucestershire
Printed in the United Kingdom

# Contents

## Acknowledgements

Latin America Bureau would like to thank Matthew Terdre, Shafik Meghji, David Treece and David Lehmann for their invaluable contributions to the book and express their gratitude to Sue Cunningham (http://www.scphotographic.com/), Julio Etchart (http://www.julioetchart.com/), Ali Rocha (www.alfixit.com), South American Pictures (http://www.southamericanpictures.com/), Christian Tagni (http://christiantragni.com/), and Survival International (http://www.survivalinternational.org/) for their help with the photographs.

Thanks are also due to Mark Perryman, from Philosophy Football, (http://www.philosophyfootball.com/), who has played a key role in bringing this view of the other Brazil to a new audience.

# Map of Brazil

# Introduction

Behind the clichés about Brazil – the Carnival, the beaches, *bossa nova* and beautiful girls, and being the country to escape to in Hollywood movies or train robbers' dreams – there is a much more interesting country, full of contrasts and contradictions, a country that is in many ways a paradox.

Brazil has largely avoided the religious, ethnic, and racial conflicts that tear other countries apart. This melting pot of indigenous, African, European, and Asian peoples has, most of the time, worked. Except for a few thousand of the more remote indigenous communities, everyone speaks one language: Portuguese. The borders are peaceful – the last time Brazil went to war with a neighbour was in 1865 against Paraguay, and since then it has settled all disputes through diplomacy. It is the only BRIC (Brazil, Russia, India, China) nation that is not a nuclear or military power. A founder member of the United Nations, it has long had a foreign policy based on non-intervention.

The paradox is that, while it practises peace abroad, Brazil is a country of horrifying interpersonal violence, with up to 50,000 Brazilians, mostly young men, mostly black, murdered every year. Extrajudicial killings, police death squads, militias and drug gangs account for most of these deaths. Brazil's youth murder rate is 273 times that of England and Wales. In the words of Amnesty International's Brazil director, Brazil seems to suffer from 'an epidemic of indifference' towards murder, especially of young men who are poor and black. There are also high rates of violence against women, against gays, and against Indians. Slave labour is still found on many ranches in the Amazon region, and clandestine loggers and miners continue to invade indigenous reserves and conservation areas with impunity.

Impunity, a key to much of what is wrong with Brazil, is aggravated by an overburdened, painfully slow, complex justice system, which ends up favouring those with money rather than those with right on their side, the perpetrators rather than the victims, the corrupt rather than the honest.

This archaic situation is in contrast to Brazil's considerable economic success – it is now the world's seventh-largest economy. It also has the biggest, most successful poverty-reduction programme in the world, which has taken millions of people out of extreme misery and turned them into consumers. Brazilian scientists are innovative and inventive, and scores of top UK and American universities now run joint programmes with their Brazilian counterparts. Brazilians are among the world's top users of social media. The country bursts with creativity, which even the sometimes Kafkaesque red tape cannot subdue.

In Brazil, yesterday's world competes with tomorrow's world. This is what makes it at the same time fascinating and appalling, delightful and dreadful, but never dull.

Military policeman surveying Rocinha favela in Rio de Janeiro (Christian Tragni)

## ESSENTIAL PORTUGUESE FOR BRAZIL

*Oi* = Hi, Hallo or what ?
*Ciao* = Bye
*Até* = see you later
*Obrigado* = Thank you (men)
*Obrigada* = thank you (women)
(N.B. Obrigado/a can also mean – No thanks – when used in
  answer to a question.)
*Por favor* = Please
*Como?* What? (do you mean)
*Tudo bem* = fine, OK, it's all right, **or** is everything OK? No
  worries? (ubiquitous phrase used as both statement and
  question, depending on inflection)
*Legal* = fine, good, OK
*Muito legal* = great
*Beleza* = great
*Quanto?* How much
*Onde?* Where
*Quando?* When
*Sim* = Yes
*Não* = No
*Nossa!* = Heavens!
*Droga!* = Dam!
*Puxa/puxa vida!* = Really! Fantastic! You don't say!
*Sou* = I am. For example, *sou inglês/inglêsa* – I am English, *sou
  americano/a* (American), *sou australiano/a* (Australian), *sou
  holandês/a* (Dutch). Remember the final letter 'o' is for males
  and 'a' is for females.
*Meu nome é* = my name is:
*Fala inglês?* = do you speak English?
*Não falo português* = I don't speak Portuguese
*Quero* = I want. For example, *quero uma cerveja* (a beer), *um
  suco* (a juice), *um café* (a coffee)
*Onde está o banheiro* = where is the toilet? Signs might say:
  *Ele* = He and *Ela* = She, or
*Homens* = Men and *Mulheres* = Women
*Com licença* = excuse me (if stuck in a crowded bus and you
  need to get to the door, it works like magic)
*Desculpe* = sorry (if you tread on someone's toe while doing so)

The King of Football, Pelé (Sue Cunningham)

# 1 Football[1]

Ecstatic fans in vast stadiums. Carefree kickabouts on golden beaches. The unmistakeable yellow shirts. *Jogo bonito* ('beautiful game'). Brazilian football evokes many images, but the country's relationship with the sport is far more complex than the clichés suggest. Since its introduction in the 1890s, football has not only entertained but been made use of to exclude and to control.

When Brazil became a republic in 1889, it was a country of more than three million square miles and around ten million people. Most of the population were illiterate and disenfranchised, and slavery had only just been abolished. Although Brazil had a monarchy, which may explain why it did not split into different countries, more was needed to weld together this disparate assortment of peoples, interests and influences. Football helped to provide this, and became a national passion.

### 'The English invented it, Brazilians perfected it'
*(old Brazilian saying)*

Fable has it that in 1894 Charles Miller, the Brazilian-born son of a Scottish rail engineer, returned from his schooling in England with a football tucked under his arm and went on to ignite Brazil's infatuation with football. Miller organized matches of this strange new game, as did another son of British immigrants, Oscar Cox, who founded Brazil's first football club, Fluminense, in 1902.

At the outset, football in Brazil was the leisure pursuit of privileged Anglo-Brazilians, who did not appreciate their 'noble game' being played by the largely non-white lower classes, and did their best to prevent others from playing or even watching the sport. The elite's determination to keep football for the white and rich was rooted as much in an attempt to maintain the status quo as in racist Victorian attitudes. In 1888 Brazil was the last country in

---

1  This chapter was written by Shafik Meghji and Matthew Terdre

the Americas to abolish slavery and, by the time football arrived, the country had a growing underclass largely made up of former slaves. The elite, who had retained most of their privileges, were eager to find something to demonstrate their difference from the hoi polloi. Football appeared to fit the bill.

However, the ease with which the game could be understood and played made it difficult for the privileged class to keep the new sport to itself. By 1910 makeshift pitches had sprung up across Brazil, as informal kickabouts took place on streets and spare pieces of land, with oranges or rolled-up socks for balls.

In a last-ditch attempt to keep out the underclass, Brazil's official clubs insisted that players must be amateurs and have another source of income, largely ruling out black players from poorer backgrounds. Mixed-race players who managed to join official clubs were subjected to racist abuse and vilification; Fluminense gained its nickname, *pó de arroz* (rice powder), because a mixed-race player, Carlos Alberto, used to whiten his skin with rice powder before matches in an attempt to fit in.

It was not until Vasco da Gama, Rio's Portuguese club, started picking players because of their ability rather than their race that the white elite's grip on the game began to loosen. According to Alex Bellos, in his book *Futebol, The Brazilian Way of Life*, Vasco got round the insistence on amateur status by employing their

(Julio Etchart)

players in the shops and factories of Rio's Portuguese community. When the elite clubs responded by insisting that players know how to write their own names in order to play in matches – a test that most of Vasco's illiterate players failed – the club organized literacy lessons and got many players to shorten their long names, starting the tradition of Brazilian players using abbreviations or nicknames.

Bellos argues that football's racist origins also helped to forge the Brazilian style of play: black players who came up against white players used dribbling and other improvised skills to avoid physical contact with their opponents and the retaliation that could be expected to follow.

### Brasil tetracampeão

A 2–0 victory by a team of São Paulo and Rio's best players over visiting Exeter City in 1914 is generally considered Brazil's first international match, but it was not until 1938 that the power of football as a unifying national force was fully realized. President Getúlio Vargas, who had come to power on the back of an uprising in 1930, centralized the sport, creating a national football council and funding Brazil's trip to the 1938 World Cup in France. There, for the first time, Brazil made it past the first

Fans at Flamengo versus Fluminense football derby in Maracanã stadium (Julio Etchart)

## THE KING AND THE LITTLE BIRD

If you had to sum up Brazilian football in one word it would be Pelé: the only player to have played in three winning World Cup teams; scorer of over a thousand goals; acclaimed as the greatest footballer of all time; named 'Athlete of the Century' by the International Olympic Committee; popularly known as *o Rei* (the King). Since retiring, Edson Arantes do Nascimento, to use his real name, has been Minister of Sport, a UN ambassador, a successful businessman, and even the face of Viagra.

But while Pelé remains a global icon, Brazilians tend to have more affection for his counterpart Manuel Francisco dos Santos, better known as *Garrincha*, the 'Little Bird'. Born with curvature of the spine, a right leg that bent inwards and a shorter left leg that bent outwards, *Garrincha* turned his deformities into assets, becoming the most mesmerising dribbler in the history of the game. He played in Brazil's winning World Cup team in both 1958 and 1962, and was named player of the tournament at the latter.

Demons, however, accompanied the gifts. A lifelong alcoholic and philanderer (he fathered at least 14 children), *Garrincha* ended up destitute and alone. He died in 1983 of cirrhosis of the liver, aged just 49. Despite the tragic elements of his life, *Garrincha* is remembered for his talents on the pitch. As Uruguayan author Eduardo Galeano wrote: 'In the entire history of football no one made more people happy.'

round, eventually reaching the semi-finals. The team and its style of play were personified by centre-forward Leônidas, who became Brazil's first football hero (whom many Brazilians credit with inventing the bicycle kick). The national team, or *seleção*, became a symbol that all Brazilians could understand and get behind.

Amateurism collapsed in Brazil in the early 1930s, thanks largely to the introduction of professional contracts by European clubs, which meant that Brazilian clubs risked losing their players unless they paid them. By 1933, São Paulo and Rio had professional leagues, with one Rio club, Bonsucesso, fielding a team of eleven black players in its inaugural year. Football was finally open to all Brazilians.

The rising importance of Brazil as a power in football was recognized in 1950, when the country was chosen to stage the first FIFA World Cup after the Second World War. The famous Estádio do Maracanã was built in Rio for the tournament, and on 16 July 1950 some 200,000 spectators crowded into it, expecting to see the national team defeat Uruguay in the final and take the Jules Rimet trophy. However, Uruguay won 2–1, sparking tears, heart attacks and even some suicides among fans.

The next World Cup was held in Switzerland in 1954. Brazil was again one of the favourites. This time they were knocked out by Hungary, in what went down in football history as the infamous 'Battle of Berne'. Three players were sent off, and the Brazilian team and supporters invaded the Hungarian dressing-room after the match, keen to continue the fight. The Brazilians were called 'animals' for their behaviour, and over

Young footballers on Ipanema Beach, Rio de Janeiro (Douglas Engle)

## THE LANGUAGE OF FOOTBALL

Many football terms are now used in everyday conversation in Brazil; here are some of the most common.

- **bola fora** = a mistake (literally, a ball outside the goal)
- **bola para frente** = to carry on (literally, to kick the ball forward)
- **pisar na bola** = to commit a gaffe (literally, to tread on the ball)
- **show de bola** = a brilliant or clever answer, performance, etc. (literally, a display of skill with the ball)
- **matar no peito** = to solve (problem, puzzle) immediately (literally, to stop – kill – the ball with your chest)
- **driblar** = to evade, get round (imported from English into Brazilian football and into everyday conversation)
- **dar um chapéu** = to find a way round a problem (literally, to give a hat; it is used in Brazilian football when a player kicks the ball over an adversary's head)
- **tirar o time do campo** = to desist (literally, to take the team off the field)
- **aos 45' do segundo tempo** = at the eleventh hour (literally, at the 45th minute of the second half)
- **deu zero a zero** = nothing happened (literally, the result was 0–0)
- **tapetão** = to solve a problem by appealing to a higher authority (literally, on the carpet, it refers to the way a football dispute is resolved off the field by a football authority)
- **Bater na trave** = to have a near miss (literally, to hit the goalpost)
- **GOOOOOOOOOOOOOOOOOOL!** = Goal!

the following decades this negative view of Latin American teams prevailed.

The *seleção*'s hour arrived at last in 1958 in Sweden. Their victory owed much to the arrival of a new star: Edson Arantes do Nascimento, better known as Pelé. Only 17 at the time of the tournament, the Brazil number 10 scored two goals in the final against the home team, and Brazil went on to win 5–2.

Brazil won again in 1962, but it is the dazzling team of the 1970 tournament that is widely considered the greatest of all time. Jairzinho, Rivelino, Tostão and, of course, Pelé inspired the *seleção* to a third victory, the footage of which – broadcast around the world in colour for the first time – helped to cement the iconic status of the team in the yellow shirts.

The *seleção* of the 1982 World Cup, featuring the likes of Zico, Sócrates and Falcão, gained almost as much adulation, although it was knocked out in the second round by the more defensive and pragmatic Italians. Brazil went on to win the 1994 and

Demonstration in Rio against the World Cup in June 2013 (Ali Rocha)

2002 World Cups, though never with quite the same attacking verve. If football is sometimes a matter of life and death in Brazil, it is also a commodity. Brazilian football is a potent brand, used to sell everything from sporting goods to holidays, and thousands of Brazilian footballers have been exported to play in foreign leagues.

The sport has also made fortunes and political careers. During the military regime, giant stadiums were built across the country in an attempt to bolster political support for the government. Corruption scandals, rigged matches and bribed referees in the domestic leagues are common, and many of the clubs and federations have been run by the same officials for decades. Known as *cartolas* (literally 'top hats'), these officials enjoy immense power and prestige and have become wealthy men. Election candidates still make donations to local teams in exchange for votes.

However, football is also a means of challenging the status quo. During an international match in Paris in 1978, for example, TV cameras could not help showing the giant banners unfurled by Brazil supporters in the crowd calling for an amnesty for political prisoners. Several players have been prominent political activists, notably Sócrates, an outspoken pro-democracy campaigner during the military dictatorship.

In 2013, as the *seleção* made unexpected progress towards the final of the Confederations Cup – an international association football tournament for national teams, currently held every four years by FIFA – hundreds of thousands of Brazilians poured on to the streets to protest about growing inequality, corruption and poor public services. Broken government promises that public money would not be used to fund the huge expense of building new stadiums – several of which were built in remote cities without a prominent local team or even much of local football tradition – and infrastructure for the 2014 World Cup meant that public anger was also directed towards FIFA and the football establishment.

Demonstrations were organized to coincide with Brazil matches, and signs began to appear warning people not to go to World Cup matches, and demanding that public money be spent on schools, hospitals and public transport instead of on stadiums that most Brazilians would never enter as they wouldn't be able to afford the tickets. Many superstar members of the *seleção* belatedly threw their support behind the protests, perhaps shocked that football, previously untouchable, was suddenly playing second fiddle to the concerns and rights of ordinary people.

## Women's football

The most talented woman footballer in the world is Marta Vieira da Silva, a Brazilian chosen FIFA World Player of the Year five times and known as 'Pelé in skirts'. But the national women's team has received little encouragement from Brazil's football authorities. Between 1965 and 1982, women were banned altogether from the game. But recent signs are more hopeful: a new women's football league of 20 teams began in December 2013, with funding from a state bank, and Brazil has decided to bid for the 2019 Women's World Cup. Brazil's Sports Minister Aldo Rebelo was determined: 'If we don't get it for 2019, then we'll have to look at another year, possibly 2023.' Could it be that the macho world of Brazilian football is at last going to make space for women?

(Douglas Engle)

Filhos de Gandhi bloc snaking through the spectators during Carnival in Salvador (Sue Cunningham)

# 2 Culture

Brazilian culture is spectacularly vibrant and rich, something that is no doubt a consequence of the country's huge geographical and ethnic diversity, and the enormous social and economic upheavals it has undergone, from the impact of colonialism and slavery, through successive waves of modernization, to its contemporary prominence in the globalized world. At the level of popular culture, African and Amerindian traditions lie at the heart of Brazilian music, dance, popular religion and a huge array of regional and local festivities. But Brazil has also produced some of the most radical and influential experimental movements in the arts, from the avant-garde modernist poets, painters, composers and prose writers of the 1920s, such as Mário de Andrade, Heitor Villa-Lobos and Oswald de Andrade, with his theory of 'cultural cannibalism', to the innovators in the visual and performance arts in the years since the Second World War, such as the Concretists and Neo-Concretists, Augusto Boal's Theatre of the Oppressed, and the Tropicalistas.

Although less known abroad, a strong tradition of fiction and poetry is belatedly reaching non-Brazilian audiences in translation, and it includes world-class names such as Machado de Assis, Carlos Drummond de Andrade, João Guimarães Rosa, Clarice Lispector and João Cabral de Melo Neto. At every step, Brazilian culture has brought together a deep sense of local, regional and national identities, a cosmopolitan appetite for international innovation and a magical ability to incorporate, synthesize and recreate in fresh, original ways.

## Search for identity

The search for a distinctive Brazilian identity to replace the prevailing Eurocentrism of art and politics permeated much of the 20th century's literature, art and music. Indigenous and black culture were rediscovered and the dehumanization of the modern industrial world rejected. Out went waltzes and polkas, in came the samba. Erudite composer Heitor Villa-Lobos wove the popular rhythms and melodies of the *choro* into his music and created the famous *Bacchianas Brasilianas*. Mário de Andrade wrote *Macunaíma*, the story of an anti-hero. Based on a legend of the Makuxi Indians, *Macunaíma* is an outrageous, amoral trickster and survivor who lives on his wits and so was seen as a fitting hero for modern Brazilians. For some, the book was also the first example of what was to become Latin America's most successful literary export, magical realism. The Week of Modern Art, first held in 1922 to mark 100 years of independence, became a landmark annual event.

In 1928 Tarsila do Amaral painted her famous *Abaporu*, launching the Anthropophagic Movement, intended to 'swallow' European culture, subvert its oppressive colonial power and turn it into something culturally very Brazilian, just as cannibals ate their enemies in order to absorb their qualities. In the 1940s and 1950s Cândido Portinari, inspired by the Soviet Union's social realism, painted workers in the coffee plantations or at the docks, and refugees fleeing the drought, making the ordinary man and woman the centrepiece of his art. He also painted two giant panels, *War and Peace*, for the UN headquarters in New York, before dying of paint poisoning.

In the 21st century, Brazil's search for its own identity continues, as the country's economic performance far outstrips its achievements in the fields of social and human development. Is it moving into the elite band of rich countries or is it still a developing country?

## Music

It's hard to do justice to the range and richness of Brazilian music. On the one hand, there is the core music of Brazil's popular traditions, such as the intensely polyrhythmic, percussive *batucada* and *maracatu*, descended from Congolese slave traditions, and their Yoruba equivalent in the Blocos Afro of Bahia; the upbeat accordion-based dance music called *forró*, and *sertaneja* – Brazil's country music; and any number of variants of samba: from the improvised, small-ensemble songsmiths of *partido alto* and carnival-style *samba-enredo*, to samba rock and samba reggae. At the same time, an endless dialogue since the early 20th century with contemporary and international currents, from Caribbean beats to European electronica and US hip-hop, makes for an amazingly dynamic and varied scene, with ever-changing hybrid styles. The internet has given musicians and singers in the far corners of Brazil access to sounds, trends and instruments they never knew about before. Recently, this explosion of internationalized voices and hybrid styles has created a powerful soundscape for a discontented youth movement to speak critically of social and political issues, just as a previous generation did in the 1960s. In a country where until recently so few people could read, music is an important form of communication; the result is that jingles, whether for politicians during elections or for consumer products, are ever present on radio stations.

While *bossa nova* turned into a global sensation after Tom Jobim's song 'The Girl from Ipanema' became an international hit in 1964, a second wave of left-wing protest singers, including Edu Lobo, Nara Leão, Geraldo Vandré, Baden Powell and Chico Buarque, politicized the new music to call for grassroots reforms and to oppose the recently installed dictatorship. Then came the Jovem Guarda, a youth pop movement whose main exponent was Roberto Carlos, inspired by American rock and the Beatles, focusing on dreams of a better material life, ignoring the political reality.

But in 1967, three years after the military had taken power by force, a group of talented musicians from Bahia, among them Gilberto Gil, Gal Costa, Tom Zé, and brother and sister Caetano Veloso and Maria Bethânia, brought the *Tropicália* movement to Rio and São Paulo and ignited a brief cultural revolution. With a provocative, libertarian fusion of Brazilian and international influences, embracing electric rock and pop, the Tropicalistas' music, lyrics and entire attitude challenged conformity and conservatism (of both the right and left). When they began singing overtly political songs like 'É Proibido Proibir' (It's Forbidden to Forbid), many of them were arrested, imprisoned or exiled.

### New voices

In the 1970s, the so-called *música popular brasileira* (MPB) tradition – which emerged out of *bossa nova*, the protest songs of the 1960s and *Tropicália* – continued to innovate and to speak of democratic values, now in the face of state censorship and repression. Many regional singers and initiatives appeared and made their names on the national scene, notably Milton Nascimento and the Clube da Esquina from Minas Gerais, and Moraes Moreira and the Novos Baianos from Bahia, while in São Paulo the Vanguarda Paulista and in Rio Hermeto Paschoal experimented radically with their own vocal and instrumental projects.

In the 1980s, with MPB on the wane, and economic and social crisis heralding the end of the military regime, a younger generation found its own voice of dissent in heavy rock, which became the dominant sound in cities such as Brasília and Belo Horizonte. In the north-eastern state capital of Salvador da Bahia, meanwhile, a black renaissance, inspired by the last of the African liberation movements and by Caribbean reggae and Rastafarianism, created another hybrid, samba reggae, as the voice of Afro-Bahian pride and militancy. In the 1990s it was the turn of *mangue beat*, a musical and cultural movement led by Chico Science and his band Nação Zumbi in Recife, which mixed local rhythms and modern music, or, as one fan put it, 'took a dive into the rich folklore of the Brazilian north-east'.

The 1990s also began to see the spread into the mainstream of *baile funk* music, which had begun some years before in the Rio *favelas*, or shanty towns, with songs that expressed the social and cultural issues of their (mostly) Afro-Brazilian

Capoeira is a well-known Brazilian martial art, developed by descendants of African slaves, which combines dance, acrobatics and music (Julio Etchart)

inhabitants. Poverty, human dignity, racial pride, violence and injustice, but above all sexual questions, were the themes. *Baile funk* was originally derived from American freestyle and Miami bass, based on electronic beats. It is now recognized as one of the first new genres of electronic street dance music to have become important outside the USA and Europe, with its peculiar combination of music, social issues, and very strong sexual appeal.

Hip hop had arrived in Brazil in the 1980s, born out of street parties, becoming a major cultural force among marginalized youth in São Paulo and other major towns, through rapping, graffiti and breakdancing. The latest development in an ever-evolving genre are *saraus*, a term once applied to genteel musical evenings in the drawing rooms of the gentry, now referring to gatherings in city peripheries, where the history of black consciousness is spread through public readings of the works of black revolutionaries such as Malcolm X and the participants' own rap poetry, which protests against police violence, prison conditions and racism. With a political, sometimes revolutionary message, today's best known hip-hop group, Racionais MC, mixes rap with samba, soul, reggae, *bossa nova*, acid-jazz, poetry and rock.

## Carnival

The Rio Carnival is the biggest song and dance spectacle in the world, with a strong element of Roman circus, as the rich and the famous, ministers, presidents, sports stars, film idols, tycoons, bankers and playboys banquet and booze the night away in luxurious boxes overlooking the *sambódromo*, the purpose-built parade ground where the samba schools perform.

Down below, hour after hour, to the hypnotic and deafening beat of hundreds of drummers and percussion players, thousands of exuberantly dressed dancers twirl, gyrate, leap, and sway. The TV cameras focus on the near-naked women, but each school has up to 3,000 *sambistas* dressed in rich costumes of plumes, sequins, and satins. It is hard to believe that once Carnival is over, the 18th-century courtiers, Indian warriors, Egyptian pharaohs, fictional characters and spacemen will metamorphose back into maids, bus drivers, labourers, shop assistants and rubbish collectors.

The samba schools began in the *favelas*, and each school still draws most of its members from one *favela* community. But celebrities, TV stars, models or soccer players are invited to 'appear' with the school, and middle-class Brazilians and even tourists increasingly buy themselves a 'Carnival experience', their less-than-expert samba steps mercifully hidden in the general melee. Behind the four-day parade lie months of rehearsals and an extraordinary amount of research into each school's theme, often used to satirize historical or current events. One winner, Imperatriz Leopoldinense, dug up a little-known episode about the decision of 19th-century Emperor Pedro II to import camels to cope with a devastating drought in the north-east. But the camels died, while the local donkeys survived, allowing an ironic reflection on the superiority of the underrated home-grown product.

The satire sometimes becomes surreal: where else would torture become a Carnival theme? A few years ago the Santa Cruz school, celebrating the 25th anniversary of the satirical newspaper *Pasquim*, fervently critical of the military regime, produced a float carrying gigantic torture instruments. Around the float danced 25 dwarfs dressed as generals.

The conservative church has frequently criticized the excesses of Carnival. Once, the Rio archbishop went to court to stop a

Rio Carnival (Julio Etchart)

replica of the Corcovado Christ statue being put on a float. The answer of carnival director Joãosinho Trinta was to wrap it in black plastic so that nobody could see it, although everyone knew what it was. It was the late Trinta who coined a phrase that became famous in answer to criticisms of the extravagant luxury of his floats and costumes: 'Intellectuals like poverty, the people want luxury.'

As Carnival grew more sumptuous and was transmitted live by the major TV channels, so commercial interests became more intrusive. Advertising by Brazil's beer companies is everywhere. For all that, one of the great delights of the Rio Carnival is still the juxtaposition of the ordinary and the fantastic – the sight of a group of Roman legionaries going home by bus, or a couple of the older women, the *baianas,* clambering into a car in their vast crinolines.

## The animal numbers game (jogo do bicho)

If you see a man sitting at a small table outside a bar, or in the shade of a tree, apparently without anything to sell, you can be sure he is taking bets for Brazil's mysterious, clandestine *jogo do bicho,* the animal game. During the day a steady stream of people come up to him, discreetly hand over some money, and he writes a number down on a slip of paper. If you get close enough, you might hear the words 'butterfly' or 'elephant'.

It all began 100 years ago, when the owner of the Rio zoo ran out of money to feed the inmates and started a raffle, based on the animals, to raise funds. It soon became a craze and the zoo was packed, not with animal lovers, but with gamblers. The game grew so popular that it spread to the streets and all over the country. The authorities attempted without success to ban the new national obsession, which has flourished ever since. It is said that 60,000 people work for the *jogo do bicho* in Rio alone, and the annual turnover is put at US$2 billion.

The game is now more sophisticated, but is still a lottery based on 25 animals and the total honesty of the bookies, as no receipts are given. The *jogo do bicho* has become part of Brazilian culture – if you dream of snakes or monkeys, forget the psychological interpretations but go and bet on your particular animal. Yet what for millions is just an innocent flutter also has its more sinister side. *Jogo do bicho's* economic power soon attracted the gambling mafia, and the bosses, known as *bicheiros*, spread their interests to illegal gambling, slot machines and drug trafficking. Often presenting themselves as benefactors of local communities, who sponsor samba schools and local soccer teams, they have a darker side involving violence and crime.

## Social media

As Brazilians have acquired more disposable income, they have become internet users in a big way. In September 2013, 80 million Brazilians were going online, either on computers or via smartphones and tablets. Users now include poorer sections of the population – shanty-town dwellers in Rio, for example, where nine out of ten of those under 30 now access the internet.

Only the US surpasses them in the use of Twitter, Facebook and YouTube. (Oddly enough, it was a Brazilian, Eduardo Saverin, who helped to found Facebook by providing Mark Zuckerberg, his fellow student at Harvard, with money in the very early days.) Brazilians are the world's keenest users of social media, with the average number of 'friends' on Facebook (known just as 'Face') higher than in any other country. Studies show that certain national characteristics help to explain this fascination: Brazilians are very sociable, they adore novelty, they prize status symbols, they like informality and they love to observe other people's lives. They enjoy showing off and demonstrating to their friends that they are doing well. Almost the exact opposite of the British, in fact. One thing they do share with the British is a well-developed sense of humour. For *Forbes* magazine, Brazil represents 'the future of the social media'.

But the fascination with social media has not cut Brazilians off from the world around them. In June 2013 the digital generation, generally criticized for its apathy, took to the streets en masse in giant protests for better public services, organized via social media. Defiant demonstrators carried a huge banner proclaiming 'we are the social media'. Another said: 'We have come out of Facebook'. And while the traditional media floundered, taken by surprise by the scale of the protests, the new Ninja (*Narrativas Independentes, Jornalismo e Ação*) Media, reporting by smartphone from the middle of the crowds, came into its own, revealing the indiscriminate use of violence by the police and the actions of the previously unknown anarchists, the Black Blocs.

## Media

Illiteracy dropped to less than 9 per cent in 2012, as more and more children were enrolled at school, but almost 20 per cent of the adult population was still functionally illiterate, able to do little more than write their names. Although the greater affluence of the last few years led to a temporary boom in newspaper readership, most people now get their news online, via smartphones, TV or radio, and the future of print journalism is as bleak as in other countries.

TV is still the dominant medium, with the supremacy of the commercial network, Globo, now being challenged by other terrestrial networks such as Record or SBT, while cable networks are widely viewed. For decades Globo was the all-powerful kingmaker of presidents and mouthpiece of governments, and has been widely accused of slanting the news to favour the establishment. The most recent example was the non-stop live coverage of the 2013 Supreme Court trial of leaders of the ruling PT, who were accused of corruption in a scandal known as the *mensalão*. After weeks of trial, they were eventually sentenced and sent to prison. In contrast, corruption scandals involving members of the opposition PSDB have received very little coverage.

Boy uses free wifi in Rio favela (Ali Rocha)

Globo's predominance owes a lot to its fast-moving, often humorous, sometimes satirical, but always sexy soap operas, which can be seen in Russia, Cuba, China and Angola as well as in the more obvious export market, Portugal. Internationally, TV Globo ranks fourth among the world's television networks, with almost as many employees as the BBC. Although TV and radio concessions are free, they carry no public service obligations. That is left to the impoverished state TV channels.

## Graffiti

The 'voice of the walls', as one paper called it, has become an outlet for protest, especially in São Paulo, a city where the vast population of the periphery lives with second-class services and permanent police violence. Here, unlike in any other area of art, cultural influences from the centre and the periphery mix. Graffiti artists exchange information via social networks, and work together on the same walls in collective paintings. The graffiti movement took off in São Paulo when the city began offering blank canvases – the walls of derelict buildings, the concrete spaces under road viaducts and tunnels, and the high walls of the wealthy classes' security-obsessed condominiums. In working-class public housing projects, like the east side's Cidade Tiradentes, a collective called *5 Zonas* began using the featureless walls of the blocks as its canvas for portraying the lives of the predominantly black residents.

In spite of the international recognition achieved by some of the graffiti artists, such as *os gêmeos* (the twins) and Francisco Rodrigues da Silva, known as Nunca, who have exhibited at the Tate Modern in London, the city authorities have often reacted boorishly, covering colourfully painted walls with coats of grey paint, obliterating works of art. While much graffiti is increasingly seen as art, as in the alleyway called Beco do Batman in Vila Madalena, with its 100-metre-long open-air virtual art gallery of abstract, surreal and psychedelic paintings, other graffiti, such as indiscriminate large-letter tagging, has defaced thousands of houses and buildings all over São Paulo.

## Literature

Brazil has no contemporary writer with the universal literary prestige and commercial success of Colombia's Gabriel García Márquez or Chile's Roberto Bolaño. Internationally, its best-selling author is Paulo Coelho, whose mystical romances have sold millions. But the international invisibility of Brazilian literature has more to do with the publishing industry's slowness to translate and promote writing in Portuguese than any dearth of quality, for the country can boast many names of world-leading calibre.

Belatedly, Joaquim Maria Machado de Assis (1839–1908) is now hailed as one of the great names of Portuguese-language literature. His novels were set in the Rio of the mid- to late-1800s, and he described, with subtle but devastating satire, the intimate workings of elite power, class conflict, and the corrosion of institutions in a decadent, slave-owning, patriarchal society. A man of mixed blood and humble background, Machado de Assis has been described as the most profound interpreter of the dying days of Brazil's empire. His best known works are *Memórias Póstumas de Brás Cubas*, (Posthumous Memories of Brás Cubas, also translated as Epitaph of a Small Winner) *Dom Casmurro* and *Quincas Borba* (Philosopher or Dog?).

Another turn-of-the-century classic was Euclides da Cunha's *Os Sertões* (Rebellion in the Backlands), published in 1902, which described the Republican state's war of annihilation against the north-eastern community of Canudos, whose inhabitants were viewed as ignorant religious fanatics standing in the way of progress. Sent by a Rio newspaper to cover the military campaign against the rebels, da Cunha found that his racist prejudices towards the 'primitive' rebels of Canudos strained against the reality of the war, which instead revealed them to be courageous men and women, defending themselves against the barbarism of the Republican forces who claimed to be upholding law, order and civilization.

Twentieth-century Brazilian literature took up the search for a Brazilian identity, and also da Cunha's cry of protest against the country's abuse and neglect of its own forgotten or despised masses. In the 1930s and 1940s, coming from different regions of the country, Graciliano Ramos wrote about the drama of the drought in *Vidas Secas* (Drylands); Jorge Amado about the exploitation on the cacao plantations and the homeless children of Salvador in *A Terra do Sem Fim* (Violent Land) and *Capitães da Areia* (Captains of the Sands); and Erico Verissimo about the fratricidal struggles in 19th century Rio Grande do Sul in his trilogy *O Tempo e o Vento* (Time and the Wind).

From Minas Gerais came João Guimarães Rosa, considered one of Brazil's greatest novelists, who took the exploration of rural life, the tension between the traditional and the modern, and the re-invention of the Portuguese language in completely new directions. Nominated for the Nobel Prize for Literature in 1967, he died before the prize was awarded and so was eliminated. His most famous work is *Grande Sertão: Veredas* (The Devil to Pay in the Backlands), published in 1956, in which he narrated the epic drama of feuding gunmen battling among the forces of good and evil, God and the Devil, in the mythical landscape of Brazil's badlands or wilderness, the *sertão*.

The other towering literary figure of the 1950s and 1960s is Clarice Lispector, a Jewish immigrant who was born in the Ukraine and died in 1977. Lispector's unique mix of poetic prose, philosophy and existentialism, with its focus on women's struggle for self-realization, earned her a special reputation among French feminist critics. Her posthumously published novella *A Hora da Estrela* (The Hour of the Star), adapted for the cinema by Suzana Amaral, is an extraordinary meditation on poverty, citizenship and the power and responsibility of the literary imagination.

Since the 1980s, much of the best Brazilian fiction has focused on the dramas of contemporary urban life – its challenges, alienation, solitude, insecurity and violence – often with a strong sense of local or regional settings beyond the familiar scenarios of Rio de Janeiro. Caio Fernando Abreu and João Gilberto Noll took us to the cityscapes of São Paulo and Porto Alegre, in the south, Luiz Ruffato has been depicting working-class life in small town Minas Gerais, and Milton Hatoum from Manaus portrays the lives of families of Lebanese immigrants, like his own, in the Amazon's capital.

In 2003 Brazil's first international literary festival, Festa Literária Internacional de Paraty (FLIP – International Literary Festival of Paraty) – the brainchild of Englishwoman Liz Calder, editor of Bloomsbury publishing house – was held in Paraty, a picturesque colonial town on the coast near Rio, inspired by the UK's Hay Festival. It has since become an established event, attracting well-known American, European and African authors and a public of several thousand, and has spawned other literary festivals across the country.

## Cinema

Brazil's film industry has survived violent ups and downs, but is now in an extremely productive phase thanks to new forms of funding. The introduction in 1995 of the Rouanet Law, giving tax breaks to firms that backed films, was particularly important. The 1998 Walter Salles' film *Central do Brasil* won a Golden Globe, while in 2002 Fernando Meirelles' *Cidade de Deus* was nominated for four Oscars. Recent successful Brazilian films have explored the prison situation – *Carandiru* (2003) by Hector Babenco – and police corruption and violence – José Padilha's *Tropa de Elite* (2007) and *Tropa de Elite 2* (2010). One hundred and twenty six films were produced in 2013, seen by 26 million cinema-goers.

Brazil's importance as a film-producing country goes back to the 1960s, when the Cinema Novo (New Cinema) movement, which had as its slogan 'a camera in the hand and an idea in the head', began to take a critical, questioning look at Brazil's poverty and social problems, rejecting the Hollywood style. The result was Anselmo Duarte's *O Pagador de Promessas*, which won the Palme d'Or at the Cannes Film Festival in 1962, and Glauber Rocha's *Deus e o Diabo na Terra do Sol* (1962) and *Terra em Transe* (1967). The military regime's censorship put an end to the movement. While political films were banned, the state film agency Embrafilme ended up funding mostly soft porn and children's films, until it was closed down by President Fernando Collor in 1990.

## Architecture

Past, present, and future are all to be found within a few hours of each other in Brazil. The city of today is São Paulo, incessantly tearing down the past and building yet more sophisticated skyscrapers, road tunnels and shopping malls, while the tenacious *favela* dwellers cling to every bit of empty land, no matter how steep, risky, or cramped. Only ten hours away by road is Ouro Preto, a hillside town of steep, cobbled streets and baroque churches built of soapstone, still essentially the same as in its heyday during the 18th-century gold rush. Here, Tiradentes and the other rebels conspired against the Portuguese monarchy, while Aleijadinho, the mixed-race son of a slave, left his inspired mark on hundreds of church carvings and statues in and around Ouro Preto. Crippled by disease, he had to have his tools tied to his mutilated hands.

Another six hours by road from Ouro Preto (or 1 hour 20 minutes flying time from São Paulo) is the city of the future, Brasília, Brazil's third capital, built from scratch in the 1950s. Brasilia, once an empty city, has grown greatly, with well over two million inhabitants now living in it and its surrounding suburbs and satellite towns. The brainchild of President Juscelino Kubitschek, the city was planned by Lúcio Costa in the shape of an aeroplane fuselage. But the man most closely associated with Brasília is the architect Oscar Niemeyer, universally recognized as one of the great names of modern architecture. Niemeyer, a lifelong communist, died in 2011 at the age of 104. He designed many well-known buildings abroad, but it was the innovative architecture of Brasília, with its curves, ramps, and columns, that made his international reputation. For André Malraux 'the only columns comparable in beauty to the Greek columns are those of the [presidential] Palace of Alvorada'.

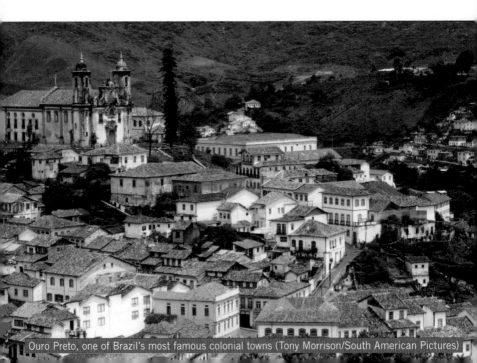

Ouro Preto, one of Brazil's most famous colonial towns (Tony Morrison/South American Pictures)

Niemeyer wanted the new capital to be an 'act of affirmation of an entire people'. But, while the palaces and congress buildings are spectacular from the outside, for those who have to work in them they fall short in functionality. Niemeyer saw Brasília as a democratic city, where rich and poor would share the advantages of a planned, healthy environment. 'Brasília was the proposal for a country that never was, created during the only moment of faith in ourselves that we've experienced in recent years', observed the poet Ferreira Gullar in the 1980s. Instead, Brasília has repeated the pattern of Brazil's older cities. The poor were expelled from the centre to the satellite towns, some of them 30 miles away. Nowadays Brasília is home to a vast bureaucracy, and annexes have been added to almost all the original government buildings to house the growing number of ministries and armies of civil servants.

## Fashion

Unsurprisingly, Brazil is the biggest market for beachware fashion. Once known for creativity more than quality, Brazilian fashion now offers both. TV soaps play a big role in popularising fashions, and growing racial awareness has seen the rise of the leggy black model alongside the wealth of Gisele Bundchen clones.

National Congress designed by Oscar Niemeyer (Sue Cunningham)

Dom Pedro I, who declared Brazil's Independence in 1822

# 3 History

Exploring the unknown world in their cramped craft, the Portuguese navigators were the astronauts of the 15th century. At Sagres, a medieval NASA built on the westernmost tip of Portugal, they perfected new navigation instruments, developed modern map-making, and calculated the circumference of the world – officially it was still flat.

In the medieval spice race, Portugal and Spain competed to find new, faster routes to the Indies, pushing back the frontiers of the known world. It is as if the monotonous European diet craved spices – pepper, nutmeg, cloves, and cinnamon – not only for their flavour, but because they were invaluable for preserving meat during the winter. Tea, sugar, chocolate, potatoes, and coffee were still unknown.

In 1500 a fleet of Portuguese ships commanded by Pedro Alvares Cabral, on its way to the east via the Cape of Good Hope, was blown off course and encountered land: by accident, Europe had 'discovered' Brazil. Baptized the 'Terra da Vera Cruz' (Land of the True Cross), the new land at first seemed disappointing: no gold or silver in sight, just lots of friendly natives, fruit, and forests. The only commercially viable product was a reddish wood. Because of its colour they called it cinder wood, *pau brasa*, and so the new land became Brasil or Brazil (the spelling varied).

A few trading posts were set up, but it was an inauspicious beginning for a country which would eventually supply the gold to finance Britain's industrial revolution, the rubber needed for the cars of the early 20th century, and the sugar and coffee that would revolutionize eating habits. Sugar soon overtook Brazil wood as the main export product and sugar plantations needed labour. The Indians who had welcomed the white man to their land were hunters and gatherers and agriculturists who worked collectively, and they resisted recruitment. Peaceful co-existence was over.

## *Indians and slaves*

Slaving expeditions were organized, and the hunters became the hunted. The indigenous population numbered at least five million when the Europeans arrived and possibly many millions more, and there is growing archaeological evidence showing that large, well-organized, and well-fed communities lived all over Brazil, including in the Amazon, and had done so for thousands of years.

(Today there are 241 indigenous nations, with 900,000 people – approximately one two-hundredth of Brazil's total population of 200 million. Almost all indigenous reserves are in the Amazon region, with only 1.5 per cent of their recognized land in the rest of Brazil.)

The Catholic missionaries who had come with the Portuguese explorers and settlers had a problem. Could the Indians be enslaved if they had souls? Did they have souls if they worshipped pagan gods and went about naked? The Jesuits decided that Indians did have souls and set about converting them, gathering thousands of Guarani Indians into fortified settlements known as 'reductions' in the south of Brazil and in Paraguay. The Indians worked the land, became literate, studied music and learnt crafts.

But the plantation owners needed slaves, not musicians, and organized raids to destroy the reductions and seize the Indians, invading Paraguay to do so. By claiming that Indians had souls, the Jesuits stood in the way of the colony's development. Accused of setting up a state within the state, they were expelled from Brazil by the Portuguese Crown in 1759, as they had been from the Spanish-speaking colonies. Priests were shipped back to Europe in chains, and the first of many attempts to build Utopia in South America ended in disaster.

The slavers were Brazil's first explorers, sailing thousands of miles up rivers in search of Indians and gold. They became known as *bandeirantes*, because they carried the flags (*bandeiras*) of their patrons on their expeditions. They were a bloodthirsty lot, killing and enslaving wherever they went – one boasted of possessing 30,000 dried human ears.

In São Paulo the word *bandeirante* acquired a heroic connotation, and there are roads, highways and monuments named in their honour. More recently, indigenous organizations and black movements have begun to question this admiration for their persecutors, and red paint to symbolize blood was thrown over the main monument.

By the 17th century, Brazil was Europe's leading sugar supplier and Portugal's most important colony. To meet the need for labour, slave ships brought across Africans in ever increasing numbers. Some historians believe that up to 13 million men, women, and children were imported during slavery's 350-year reign in Brazil, before abolition in 1888. They were counted not as individuals but by weight, as if they were merchandise, and referred to as *peças* (pieces). (Many years later the Nazis also referred to Jewish people loaded into cattle wagons for transport to the death camps as *stucken*, pieces.)

Brazil imported six times as many Africans as the United States, double the number that went to the Spanish colonies or to the British West Indies. Originally intended for the sugar plantations, the Africans ended up wherever there was economic activity. For four centuries, Brazil's immense wealth was accumulated through the work of slaves. They cut cane, panned for gold, and picked cotton and coffee. They were porters for the *bandeirantes* and tilled fields for priests and monks. In the towns, they worked as cooks, house servants, nursemaids, street sellers, sedan chair carriers, water carriers, and labourers. Slaves were the hands and feet of their masters. 'The Brazilian dream was

The Enawene Nawe are managing to continue their own way of life in modern Brazil (Fiona Watson/ Survival International)

to have one or two slaves whose labour could be hired out for a price high enough to free the dreamer from ever having to work. Begging was preferable to work. 'Even beggars had slaves', wrote Dom Pedro I, Brazil's first post-independence ruler.

When Brazil went to war against Paraguay in the War of the Triple Alliance (1865–70), slaves fought in place of their masters and, with Indians, made up the bulk of the army. They were promised freedom if they survived. The slaves came mostly from West Africa and what are now Angola and the Congo. Many were Muslim; quite a few were skilled artisans, goldsmiths, silversmiths and blacksmiths. In the gold region of Minas Gerais, they built the beautiful baroque churches that still stand today. To make rebellion more difficult, slaves were separated and dispersed among those who spoke different languages and had different customs. What united them was their suffering and their revolt at the inhuman conditions to which they were subjected. The average life span of a plantation slave was between seven and eight years.

Clóvis Moura, an Afro-Brazilian sociologist, believes that slavery left a deep imprint on Brazilian society and culture that has lasted until today. It laid the foundations for economic inequality and exploitation, influenced the way in which institutions, groups, and classes developed after abolition, and contributed to an authoritarian culture of deference and submission.

## Slave rebellion

There used to be a school of thought that considered Brazil's mixing of races, which owes its origin to the lack of white women in the colony, to have been largely peaceful thanks to the greater benevolence of the Portuguese as compared with other colonialists. Now, however, it is acknowledged that the Portuguese were as cruel as anyone else, branding, flogging and mutilating their slaves, working them until they dropped dead on the plantations. Runaways were hunted down and severely punished.

The result was constant revolts, rebellions and uprisings and the creation of hundreds of free territories, known as *quilombos*, set up by groups of runaway slaves all over Brazil. The more remote have survived until today, and under the 1988 Constitution the descendants of those runaway slaves can claim the right to the land they occupy.

## *Zumbi and Palmares*

The most famous *quilombo* was so large that it was known as the Republic of Palmares. It covered an area of 17,000 square miles in what is now the state of Alagoas. Up to 30,000 people lived in dozens of villages, as Indians and poor whites came to join the runaway slaves. The largely male population raided plantations and villages for women, but the sexual imbalance was so great that polyandry became the custom, each woman having up to five husbands.

Palmares developed its own language, a mixture of Bantu and Portuguese. The ex-slaves hunted, fished and farmed the land. They made pottery, baskets and musical instruments, wove cloth and forged iron, making weapons with which to defend themselves. For the time it lasted, from 1630 to 1695, solidarity, equality, and co-operation replaced the degradation and exploitation of the plantations.

For Brazil's rulers, however, Palmares was diabolical and dangerous, a permanent incentive to revolt which had to be destroyed, its memory erased. Supported by the church and the plantation owners, the government organized armies of *bandeirantes*, mercenaries, and criminals to do the job. In 1695, after several expeditions, Palmares was finally overrun. All the inhabitants were killed or enslaved, and the severed head of Zumbi, its legendary leader, was put on display to terrorize black Brazilians, who had come to believe that he was immortal. In a way he became so. Three hundred years later, Palmares is a heritage site, Zumbi is officially a national hero, and the date of his death, 20 November, is commemorated as National Black Consciousness Day.

Even after the most famous *quilombo* was destroyed, slaves continued to escape. In 1741 the King of Portugal ordered all runaways to be branded with the letter F for *fujão* (runaway). Newspapers in the 19th century carried columns of 'wanted' advertisements for runaway slaves, which convey an idea of the treatment they were fleeing from. The *Diário de Pernambuco* of 23 May 1839 offered a reward for a runaway called Joana, who had 'burn marks on her breasts and few front teeth'. In 1870 the same paper was looking for a slave called Germano, aged 17 or 18, 'with a sad look, big feet, long legs and marks of recent punishment on his buttocks'.

## Abolition

In 1850 the British, who had ended slavery in their own colonies, also opposed the international slave trade, and blockaded Brazilian ports. By now a third of the Brazilian population were slaves, and they continued to be smuggled in. But inside Brazil, the abolition campaign was gathering momentum, and laws were introduced to ensure the freedom of children born to slave women and to enable slaves to buy their freedom. Total abolition came only in 1888, later than in any other country in the hemisphere. By then European immigration and the release of slaves had reduced the number of slaves to just 5 per cent of the total of 14 million Brazilians.

Slave owners had predicted disaster when the traffic was banned, but the end of investment in human suffering instead freed capital for investment in infrastructure, and encouraged the immigration of free workers. But life was not easy for freed slaves. While they had been captive, land was free to anyone who occupied it; but a new Land Law changed that, turning all land into Crown or private property, in an attempt to control the former slaves' access to land.

Some slaves stayed where they were, because they had nowhere else to go. Many, abandoned without money, jobs, or homes, occupied empty land or hillsides, setting the precedent for today's occupations by landless rural workers, and shanty-town dwellers. Swiftly a vagrancy law was enacted, making anyone without a fixed address and work – the case of the ex-slaves – liable to arrest. The law survived until relatively recently, though it has not been implemented very systematically.

One of the reasons slavery lasted longer in Brazil than anywhere else in the Americas was the survival of the monarchy. Long after all the other colonies of Latin America had become republics, Brazil was ruled by an emperor. The American War of Independence and the French Revolution had been over for a century when Brazil finally became a republic in 1889.

## Tiradentes

Brazilians objected to the taxes imposed by Lisbon and resented the ban on industry or indeed learning, but all attempts to overthrow the monarchy failed. Printing presses, bookstores, universities, and foreign newspapers were forbidden. The most famous attempt at independence was in 1792, inspired by the successful French Revolution. The conspiracy foundered when the small group of plotters were betrayed and arrested, and the Crown decided to make an example of one of them, Joaquim José da Silva Xavier, a young military cadet, who was known as Tiradentes (tooth-puller) because of his off-duty activities. The hapless Tiradentes was hung, drawn, and quartered in Rio de Janeiro.

But while his fellow conspirators are forgotten, Tiradentes is now a Brazilian national hero, and his name has been given to streets, squares and palaces all over the country. He was also the only one of the conspirators for independence who thought it should also mean an end to slavery.

## Royal independence

Instead it fell to Napoleon to provoke Brazil's unique variety of royal independence. To escape from Bonaparte's triumphant advance through the Iberian peninsula in 1808, the entire royal Portuguese court and its hangers-on, a total of 15,000 people, fled to Brazil aboard a fleet of ships, led by the King Regent João VI and his mother, Queen Maria, known as Mad Maria.

Suddenly Brazil was no longer a distant colony, but the centre of the Portuguese empire, with Rio its metropolis. All around Brazil, the Spanish colonies were fighting for independence, but the presence of the monarchy gave Brazil metropolitan status, allowing it to trade directly with other countries. Universities, factories, printing presses were now allowed, and libraries, museums and botanical gardens were created.

When the Napoleonic wars were over and the King returned to Lisbon in 1821, the Portuguese tried unsuccessfully to turn the clock back and return their richest possession to colonial status.

But the King's son, Pedro, left behind as regent, soon realized that his best move would be to lead the burgeoning movement for independence rather than oppose it. Instead of the bloody warfare that ravaged other Latin American countries, Brazil became independent in 1822 – so the story goes – with a single shout beside the River Ipiranga (which became known as the *grito do Ipiranga*), when Pedro allegedly yelled his melodramatic 'Independence or Death'.

Amazingly, the Brazilian empire lasted another 67 years. Acting as a focus for loyalty and political unity, it prevented the vast country, which shared borders with ten other colonies, ex-colonies, and independent states, from breaking up. It also enabled an aristocratic white class to prolong its rule over a slave society. Brazil was free from Portugal, but millions of slaves had yet to become free citizens.

Pedro I ruled for only nine years before abdicating in favour of his son, Pedro II, who championed all the latest technological inventions, but did not see why slavery should be abolished. Under his rule, Brazil became the second country (after England) to introduce postage stamps. The Emperor was the first Brazilian to have a telephone, and encouraged the spread of the railways. Brazil was modernising, but slavery continued.

### The republic

In 1888, after a long campaign, slavery was finally abolished. By then coffee had long surpassed sugar and gold as Brazil's most

Coffee picker in Minas Gerais state (Tony Morrison/South American Pictures)

important product, and the São Paulo coffee planters had become the most powerful political and economic group in the country. They wanted a republic, and pressure grew to abolish the monarchy. The republican movement found allies among military officers who had served in the war against Paraguay and were discontent with government policy. On 15 November 1889, 'in the name of the people, the army, and the navy', Emperor Pedro II was deposed and given 24 hours to leave the country. A provisional republic, headed by Marshal Deodoro da Fonseca, a war hero, was installed.

Church and state were separated and the Republic of Brazil was formally created in February 1891 with a constitution drawn up by a Constituent Assembly. Along with the monarchy went the Catholic Church's status as the official religion. The republicans turned instead to positivism, which had been developed by the French philosopher Auguste Comte, preferring scientific rationalism to religious belief. The country's new flag, with its motto 'Order and Progress', was inspired by the new thinking.

## Antônio Conselheiro (Antônio the Counsellor)

The monarchy had gone, southern cities now had gas lighting, telephones, and electric trams, but in the north-east, the home of Brazil's first cycle of sugar wealth, little had changed. Landowners were authoritarian patriarchs, some of them despots, and most of the population lived in extreme poverty, worsened by a devastating drought in 1877. Thousands emigrated to the Amazon, where the first of several rubber booms was in full swing, or to the south. Many who stayed in the north-east starved.

Without help from the government, the landowners, or the church, people turned to mysticism. They began to follow a man with a flowing beard and rough robes who roamed the *sertão* (drylands) preaching that the end of the world would come in the year 1900. Thousands flocked to hear the charismatic Antônio Maciel, who became known as Antônio Conselheiro (Antônio the Counsellor) because of his skill as a preacher. What began as a religious movement developed into a challenge to the existing social and political system of the north-east.

Antônio Conselheiro talked about the need for a better life in the here and now. He tore down public notices announcing tax increases. The church declared him a subversive, while the state governor wanted him locked up in a mental asylum. As thousands abandoned their homes to follow the preacher, landowners feared a labour shortage. In 1893 the band was attacked by soldiers, and Antônio Conselheiro realized that he must find a sanctuary.

Like an Old Testament prophet, he led his followers on a march into the *sertão* until they came to an isolated valley surrounded by five mountain ranges. Within two years, the city they founded had become one of the largest towns in Bahia, boasting 20,000 inhabitants, two churches, and a thriving economy which even exported goatskins to Europe. It was called Canudos.

Visitors reported in wonder, 'there are neither rich or poor; the land belongs to all; there is no hunger or misery, no money, no police or thieves, no locks on doors, no brothels, no alcohol; everyone is happy in one big brotherhood.' A five-hour working day left time for prayers and leisure. There were schools for the children. Antônio Conselheiro had modelled Canudos on Thomas More's *Utopia*, which he had read.

The Brazilian establishment had no time for Utopia, especially in the backward north-east. By offering the example of a successful egalitarian society, Canudos threatened the existing system of exploitation, hunger, ignorance, and wealth for the few. Like Palmares before it, Canudos had to be destroyed before the example could spread.

In the capital, Rio de Janeiro, Canudos was used as an excuse by the military to attack the remaining monarchists. Antônio Conselheiro and his followers were portrayed as a bunch of dangerous fanatics, plotting to overthrow the republic and restore the monarchy.

Yet the apparently easy task of wiping out a backlands rebellion turned instead into the Brazilian army's biggest and bloodiest campaign since the war against Paraguay 20 years earlier. The men and women of Canudos resisted with improvised guerrilla tactics and rustic weapons, harassing the soldiers as they approached the town through the canyons and hills. It took four military expeditions more than a year to overrun Canudos, with large numbers of both soldiers and local inhabitants dying.

## The end of Canudos

The final expedition in 1897 brought together 10,000 soldiers, drawn from 11 different states, and 19 heavy cannon. As they advanced through the dry, inhospitable *sertão*, they passed the skeletons of soldiers from previous expeditions. Twelve days before the final attack, Antônio Conselheiro died. Once the government troops had taken the city, after fierce hand-to-hand fighting, they set fire to it, killed most of the survivors, and handed out the children as booty. Many ended up as prostitutes. Antônio Conselheiro's body was disinterred and his head cut off and examined, unsuccessfully, for signs of madness.

The battle for Canudos was reported in Europe, where *The Times* of London named him the 'Backlands Messiah', and criticized the manipulation of the uprising to attack monarchists. Official Brazilian history labelled Canudos a story of religious fanaticism, and in his book *Os Sertões*, which became a classic, journalist Euclides da Cunha (see Chapter 2) attributed the movement to madness brought on by racial mixing. A 12-mile-long reservoir now covers the ruins of the town. Beside it is a new town, Nova Canudos, small, poor and backward.

The Brazilian 40th Infantry battalion in Canudos, 1897

## The rubber boom

Thousands of miles west of Canudos, fortunes were being made in the Amazon rainforest: rubber was needed in Europe and America to make pneumatic tyres for motor cars. English, American, Peruvian and Brazilian companies set up trading posts along the rivers, enlisting Indians to collect the rubber, often in conditions of slavery.

The Amazon capital, Manaus, a small settlement on the edge of the river, flourished. Solid European-style buildings and an extravagantly beautiful opera house appeared among the huts and boats. Famous opera stars travelled across the Atlantic and 1,000 miles upriver to sing there. The pavement around the opera house was made from rubber tiles to muffle the sound of the horses' hooves as the carriages drew up. The rich sent their laundry to Paris, while ships brought back German sausages, Parisian hats (and clean laundry), and Polish prostitutes.

The boom lasted until 1912, when cheaper rubber, grown from thousands of saplings smuggled out of the Amazon to Kew Gardens by an Englishman called Henry Wickham, began to inundate the market. Malaya, where the saplings had flourished, soon dominated the world market, and Manaus sank back into torpor. Millions of dollars had been earned by the rubber barons at the cost of thousands of Indian lives, but little had changed.

Supplying rubber for Europe's and America's vehicles was not Brazil's only contribution to advancing technology. Competing with the Wright brothers, Alberto Santos Dumont made the first registered flight in a heavier-than-air machine in Paris in 1906. He also invented the wristwatch to keep his hands free for flying. Years later he committed suicide, grieved by the use of his invention for waging war.

### Immigration

Exports of coffee and other agricultural produce still dominated the Brazilian economy in the first few decades of the 20th century, but coffee wealth had stimulated industry, and thousands of factories were opening, attracting a flood of immigrants.

Between 1888, when slaves were freed, and 1928, 3.5 million people arrived in Brazil, principally Italians, Portuguese, Spanish, Germans and Japanese. The new expanding urban classes had more in common with their counterparts in Europe and North America than with the landowners and the dirt-poor peasantry of the countryside. Italian and Spanish anarchists soon organized in the factories and led the first strikes for better conditions, but failed to threaten the rural elites who still controlled political power.

## The Prestes column

After overthrowing the monarchy, the military continued to want more change. In 1924 an army officer named Luís Carlos Prestes led a rebellion against the federal government, demanding social and economic reforms. Persecuted by troops loyal to the government, the rebels fled to the countryside, attacking and occupying towns, marching more than 15,000 miles in three years.

The 1,500 men who began the march were devastated by cholera and eventually sought exile in Bolivia. Prestes later became Secretary General of the Brazilian Communist Party (PCB), after spending three years in Moscow. In the 1930s he was imprisoned for nine years while his wife, Olga Benário, a German Jew, was deported to die in Ravensbrück concentration camp.

## Getúlio Vargas

The rule of the rural oligarchies of São Paulo and Minas Gerais, known as the coffee-with-milk alliance, because of their respective products, was finally broken in 1930 by a man from the southern state of Rio Grande do Sul. When Getúlio Vargas' troops tethered their horses to the monuments adorning the central plazas of São Paulo and Rio, they opened a new chapter in Brazilian history.

Vargas, a former deputy, minister, and governor of Rio Grande do Sul, ruled for 15 years, first as constitutional president, then, following a failed communist uprising in 1937, as dictator. His 'New State', inspired by Italian fascism, lasted until the end of the Second World War.

Vargas reorganized the trade unions, now run by men handpicked to collaborate with the government, along corporatist lines. Strikes were banned but working conditions were improved, and labour rights introduced, including the minimum wage.

The fascist influence of the time is still visible in Brazil, not only in the structure of the trade unions, but also in some of its public buildings. In the Governor's Palace in João Pessoa, capital of Paraíba state, the ornamental tiled floor incorporates a swastika, a bizarre relic from this time.

## The Second World War

After 1937, Vargas stamped out opposition and closed Congress. Political prisoners were routinely tortured by his dreaded head of the secret police, Filinto Müller. For the first three years of the Second World War, Brazil maintained relations with the Axis powers, but in 1942 US economic pressure persuaded Vargas to allow Allied air bases on the north-east coast, the nearest point to Africa.

In retaliation, German submarines attacked Brazilian merchant ships off the coast, killing more than 600 people. Brazil declared war on Germany and sent a contingent of 25,000 men to fight with the Allies in the invasion of Italy in 1944, the only Latin American country to do so.

President Vargas at the 50th anniversary celebrations for the Brazilian republic in 1939

In the Amazon, 30,000 rubber-tappers recruited in the north-east temporarily revived the dying rubber industry to supply the Allies, who were cut off from their Asian plantations by the Japanese invasion of Malaya. Dumped in the rainforest to fend for themselves, thousands of them died from malaria, attacks by wild animals, and hunger. In exchange for Brazilian collaboration and raw materials, the USA financed the infant steel industry, and by the 1950s industry had overtaken agriculture in economic importance.

Vargas invested in infrastructure and accelerated Brazil's industrialization by establishing powerful state companies. Massive migration began from the countryside to the cities, and Brazil's population soon ceased to be predominantly rural. By the 1980s, three-quarters of the population was living in urban areas.

The post-war clamour for democracy reached Brazil, and Vargas had to resign, only to return as elected president in 1950. In his second term in office, Vargas continued to invest in infrastructure and industrialization and widened workers' benefits.

In response to nationalist demands, he created the state oil company, Petrobrás, earning the hostility of the conservative establishment and the US government. Under political and economic pressure and facing a hostile press and Congress, Vargas, once the all-powerful dictator, felt isolated.

## Putting Brazil on the map

In 1954 Vargas committed suicide, setting off a turbulent period of 40 years during which only one elected president, Juscelino Kubitschek, who succeeded Vargas in 1955, completed his term of office.

Kubitschek, whose slogan was 'fifty years in five', was an optimistic expansionist who believed in Brazil's destiny as a great country. Brasília, a brand new capital set in the flat empty plains of central Brazil, 700 miles inland from São Paulo and the old capital, Rio de Janeiro, was built in three years. To finish it on time, bricks were flown in by the plane-load. Construction workers flocked from all over the country to build Brasília, and stayed on to become the first inhabitants of the city, living in ramshackle dormitory suburbs well out of sight of the imposing futuristic buildings of the carefully planned centre.

Kubitschek also built the first highway to the Amazon, from Brasília to Belém, and encouraged foreign multinationals to open car factories in São Paulo. He put Brazil on the world map, at the cost of rapidly accelerating inflation.

Kubitschek was succeeded in 1961 by Jânio Quadros, a charismatic but eccentric populist who mixed campaigns against bikinis and horse racing with a non-aligned foreign policy, decorating Che Guevara, then Cuban minister of industry, and supporting Fidel Castro when the US launched the Bay of Pigs invasion in the same year.

## Leading up to the coup

Inflation began to get out of control, and Quadros, accused of planning a coup d'état against a hostile Congress, surprised everyone by resigning after only eight months in power, blaming 'hidden forces' for his downfall. Conservative military officers tried to stop vice-president João Goulart, regarded as a leftist, from taking office, but Goulart's brother-in-law, Leonel Brizola, governor of the state of Rio Grande do Sul, led a campaign for legalism, and eventually Goulart, a wealthy landowner who believed in social reform, was elected president.

During Goulart's three-year government, Brazil became increasingly polarized between those who wanted radical change and those who wanted to uphold the status quo, rejecting the reforms as communist-inspired. The conservative Catholic Church preached against the 'communist' threat, especially the idea of land reform. In the north-east, peasant leagues began organising under the charismatic leadership of Francisco Julião. Bands of men on horseback, armed with old shotguns, appeared demanding land reform. In the cities, army sergeants and sailors defied military regulations to hold huge rallies, demanding better pay and conditions.

## Role of the United States

The US government had always reserved for itself the right to determine economic and political policy in Latin America – its 'backyard' – using a mixture of carrot and stick. After 1945 American policies in the hemisphere were dominated by the Cold War, and, after the Cuban Revolution of 1959, by the need above all to prevent 'another Cuba'. In 1961 President Kennedy launched the Alliance for Progress, an aid and development programme designed to bind Latin American countries into an anti-communist front. Peace Corps volunteers were poured into Latin America – Brazil alone received over 600.

The US also tried to stop the threatened nationalization of foreign companies, using a combination of open economic pressure (cutting credits and refusing to renegotiate countries' foreign debts) and covert methods, such as financing local right-wing organizations. Washington wanted Brazil's agricultural policy to provide a market for US farm equipment and US exports such as wheat and dairy products. Secretary of State John Foster Dulles is alleged to have said, 'Brazilian wishes are secondary, though it is useful to pat them on the head a bit and make them think that you are fond of them.' When the United States saw its interests threatened by a pro-reform government, it began to encourage right-wingers in the army and congress to stage a military coup.

## Military dictatorship

The coup eventually came in 1964, when the army high command, supported by the conservative classes and backed by the US, overthrew Goulart, who took refuge in Uruguay. Once the generals were in command of the economy, they promoted the development of Brazilian industry behind high protectionist barriers, creating the so-called 'tripod' of state, national companies and multinational companies, which became the basis for Brazil's much-vaunted 'economic miracle'. To help the miracle along, unions were stifled, strikes banned, and wages reduced, while censorship prevented any but favourable economic news being published.

The avowed aim of what the generals christened the 'Glorious Revolution' was to 'restore democracy, reduce inflation, and end corruption'. Instead, the long-lasting military regime shattered democratic organizations, fed corruption by censoring the press, and left behind, 21 years later, a huge, unpayable foreign debt. Unlike other regional military dictators, such as Chile's Augusto Pinochet, or Paraguay's Alfredo Stroessner, the Brazilian generals stuck to four-year terms of office, succeeding each other in power.

For the USA, Brazil under military rule became an important regional leader and ally in the Cold War. Relations later turned sour, when President Jimmy Carter made human rights a prominent issue, and Brazil began to seek a more independent trade policy, looking not only to Europe and Japan but also to the Third World for markets.

During the dictatorship, over 20,000 Brazilians were imprisoned, most of them tortured – including the current president, Dilma Rousseff, then aged 19. Some were killed, and as many as 400 prisoners 'disappeared'. Thousands more went into exile, including many who later became ministers and leaders. One, Fernando Henrique Cardoso, became President in the 1990s.

Urban guerrilla groups appeared after Congress, unions, and every available democratic forum had been closed down by repression and censorship. After making an initial impact by hijacking planes, raiding banks, and kidnapping the American, German, and Swiss ambassadors and exchanging them for political prisoners, the groups were implacably hunted down and eliminated.

When 60 guerrillas moved from the cities to the Araguaia region of the Amazon basin in 1972 to begin a Maoist-inspired revolution deep in the forest, they were soon discovered. Fifteen thousand soldiers were deployed in the region, peasant farmers were intimidated and tortured for information, and all of the group were either killed or captured.

### Economic miracle

With political pacification achieved by force of arms, Brazil became the darling of foreign investors because of its economic growth, which averaged more than 10 per cent every year between 1968 and 1973. The middle classes, beneficiaries of growing income inequality, had never had it so good, while the USA recognized Brazil as an emerging world power. 'Where Brazil goes, there goes the rest of the hemisphere', President Nixon told one of the military presidents, General Emílio Médici, in 1973.

Between 1973 and 1980, Chile, Uruguay, Argentina, and Bolivia all suffered bloody military coups, and set up, with Brazil, the secret Operation Condor to exchange intelligence and prisoners and to plan the assassinations of democratic leaders.

Brazil's military had a clear geopolitical plan to turn the country into a world power, which would dominate Latin America and control the south Atlantic. The generals also intended to make Brazil a nuclear power, concluding a US$10-billion nuclear co-operation agreement with West Germany in preference to signing the Nuclear Non-Proliferation Treaty.

The military planned massive relocations of the population to secure 'empty' areas in the north and ease pressure for land reform in the south. Hundreds of thousands of small farmers in the south were encouraged to occupy the Amazon region, or to cross the border into the fertile, empty land of Paraguay. Recurring droughts in the north-east also produced armies of unemployed migrant labourers who were hired to build dams in the Amazon. After this work was completed, many became itinerant gold prospectors, who polluted the rivers and invaded Indian reserves.

## *The return to democracy*

Armed opposition had been crushed, but non-violent opposition to the regime grew steadily. Students began to organize street demonstrations in the mid-1970s. The memorial mass for murdered journalist Vladimir Herzog in October 1975 in the Cathedral in the Praça da Sé, the central square of São Paulo,

Ceremony in Brasilia in 1985 ending 21 years of military rule (Julio Etchart)

turned into a giant silent protest. Campaigns were begun for the release of political prisoners, and catholic church groups organized protests against the rising cost of living. The church also created the Comissão Pastoral da Terra (CPT – Pastoral Land Commission) to denounce the violence and expulsions taking place principally in the Amazon region. The Ordem dos Advogados do Brasil (OAB – Brazilian Bar Association) pressed for the re-establishment of the rule of law.

In 1978 the giant car factories in São Paulo's industrial suburbs were brought to a standstill as workers defied the ban on strikes to demand better wages. A charismatic new leader emerged: Luiz Inácio da Silva, known to all as Lula. In spite of police repression, the strikers held their ground, supported by the progressive church, which organized food parcels for their families and lent churches for meetings.

Brazil seethed with unrest and demands for the restoration of democracy. Within the military, there was a power struggle between a hard-line right-wing faction, who wanted to clamp down on any sort of opposition, and a more liberal faction, who realized that the time had come to begin handing power back to civilians.

In 1984 millions took to the streets in vast rallies to demand the the right to elect the president (*diretas já* – direct elections now!). Troops surrounded the congress building in Brasilia to intimidate deputies into rejecting a bill restoring free general elections.

The military, after 21 years in power, finally did hand over to a civilian government in 1985. The economy had grown in size to tenth-largest in the world, but wages, health, and education levels had failed to keep up. A decade-long 'safe, gradual' transition from military to civilian rule averted political upheaval, and an amnesty law introduced in 1979 prevented the trial of military or police personnel for human rights violations.

The military regime left behind a more unequal, more corrupt society, with weakened political institutions. The move from authoritarian regime to a politically free society was painfully slow; it came without rupture, bloodshed, show trials, or purges, but there was a price to pay. The long-drawn-out transition period gave time for numerous politicians to abandon ship, disengage themselves from the unpopular military, and present themselves instead as the opposition, where they vigorously resisted pressure for more radical reforms.

Many civilians who had served the regime without opposing its use of torture and repression remained in power: people like José Sarney, who unexpectedly became president in 1985 when veteran politician Tancredo Neves, chosen by electoral college, became ill on the eve of his inauguration and later died.

## The playboy president

Brazilians at last regained the right to elect their president in 1989. Tired of dour generals and elderly politicians, they voted in sufficient numbers for Fernando Collor, an arrogant young newcomer with a glamorous image. Supported by the powerful TV Globo network, Collor used an array of dirty tricks to overtake the PT's Luiz Inácio Lula da Silva at the last moment. Collor wowed the population with his playboy lifestyle, his mastery of the sound-bite ('I'll kill inflation with one karate chop') and his ambitious promises to modernize Brazil, bring it into the First World, smash corruption and streamline the government.

His first drastic anti-inflation measure, the confiscation for 18 months of most of the savings of everyone who had a bank account, ruined many people and plunged the economy into recession. Fidel Castro, in Brazil for Collor's inauguration, commented,

Towards the end of the military dictatorship people were demanding free elections
Tony Morrison/South American Pictures)

'Even I wouldn't have dared do that.' Eventually, accused of corruption even by his own brother, Collor was forced to resign a few minutes before Congress voted for his impeachment.

## Fernando Henrique Cardoso

Collor was succeeded by his vice-president, Itamar Franco, who chose as finance minister the sociologist Fernando Henrique Cardoso. After the high drama of Collor's presidency, Franco provided an easy-going interregnum in which the economy grew and Brazil won the 1994 World Cup. But inflation began to spiral, reaching nearly 50 per cent per month in May 1994.

Four months before the next presidential elections, a successful economic plan (the *plano real*) was introduced, and the feel-good factor of low inflation sparked a consumer boom, which won Cardoso the presidency.

Cardoso had promised constitutional reforms to denationalize state sectors and deregulate the economy, measures that were welcomed by foreign investors, bankers, and governments as a return to more orthodox policies after ten years of roller-coasting. Record interest hikes were introduced to kill off the consumer boom and damp down the risk of inflation, but the price was rising unemployment. Cardoso's hope of rising above the old habit of exchanging favours for votes proved vain. The only constitutional reform he achieved was to change the law to allow himself to stand for re-election.

On the social front, the only new initiative was the Comunidade Solidária, modelled on Mexico's solidarity programme. Run by Cardoso's anthropologist wife, Ruth, it directed government grants and food to needy communities. A scheme known as Bolsa Escola was introduced to stop widespread child labour, by giving families allowances if they sent their children to school.

## The 21st century

This century so far, after the upheavals of the previous century, has seen the predominance of the Partido dos Trabalhadores (PT – Workers' Party) in power, led first by the charismatic former trade unionist and party founder, Luiz Inácio Lula da Silva, and then by Dilma Rousseff. Without an overall majority in Congress, however, the PT has had to ditch any ideas of radical reform, and form coalition governments with other parties right across the political spectrum. It has largely stuck to orthodox economic policy, although its foreign policy has been much more independent: Brazil no longer automatically lines up behind the United States.

The most far-reaching innovation has been in social policy, where the government's poverty reduction programme (known as conditional cash transfers), which grew out of the Cardoso government's less ambitious programme, has become a model for other countries. The basis of the programme is to give small but regular cash sums to women whose income falls below a certain very low threshold, on condition that their children go to school and have regular medical check-ups.

This century has also seen the emergence of a new, upwardly mobile lower middle class, who have more disposable income, are more educated, more plugged in to social media, but still woefully under-served in basic services like health, sewerage, housing and public transport. There has also finally been a reduction in Brazil's notoriously extreme inequality, as a result of the conditional cash transfer programme as well as other policies and a growth in formal registered employment.

President Lula takes office for the second time (Wilson Dias/ Agência Brasil under Creative Commons Licence 3 http://upload.wikimedia.org/wikipedia/commons/8/88/Lula%27s_presidential_inauguration%2C_2007.jpg)

The Workers' Party, the PT, first came to power in 2002 (Julio Etchart)

# 4 Politics

Brazil has been, in less than a century and a half, a monarchy, a republic, and a federation. It has been ruled by parliament, civilian presidents, military juntas, general-presidents, and by a civilian dictator. Being President of Brazil involves a certain degree of occupational hazard. In the last 60 years, one president has committed suicide, two resigned (one to avoid impeachment), another was overthrown by a coup, and one was taken fatally ill on the eve of taking office. After Juscelino Kubitschek left office in 1961, the next elected president to complete his term was Fernando Henrique Cardoso in 1998.

The present generation of presidents has faced problems before taking office, rather than after. One was exiled for being a left-wing intellectual, another imprisoned for trade union activities, and today's president, Dilma Rousseff, the daughter of a Bulgarian immigrant, was arrested and tortured for being a member of an urban guerrilla movement.

Besides the plethora of presidents, there has been a surfeit of legislation. Since independence in 1822, seven constitutions have been approved or imposed. The latest, approved in 1988, is already being revised.

## *Weak parties*

While other Latin American countries have for generations had their Blancos and Colorados, their Liberales and Conservadores, parties in Brazil appear and disappear overnight. Politicians change parties as other people change clothes. There are at present 32 political parties. The PT (Partido dos Trabalhadores – Workers' Party), founded in 1980, is already the fourth-oldest party. Without strong parties, interest groups have taken precedence over ideologies, clientelism over the public interest.

This fragmentation of the parties has slowed the work of Congress, as each bill has to be painstakingly negotiated by the government not only with each party, but with each of its separate factions. Instead of representing an ideological position,

## THE MAIN POLITICAL PARTIES

**Partido dos Trabalhadores** (PT – Workers' Party), founded in 1980 by a group of trade union leaders and intellectuals, was the only really ideological political party in Brazil, but since it has been in power (from 2002), it has succumbed to realpolitik and formed alliances with former opponents in order to get legislation passed.

**Partido do Movimento Democrático Brasileiro** (PMDB – Brazilian Democratic Movement Party), was set up during the military regime to be the official opposition party, to maintain the fiction that there was democracy. It evolved into a real opposition, and in 1985, under President José Sarney, formed the first civilian government after the dictatorship. Numerically, it is still the biggest party in Brazil, but ideologically it is a rainbow coalition, which might vote in any way.

**Partido da Social Democracia Brasileira** (PSDB – Brazilian Social Democracy Party), also called the Tucano party after its symbol, a toucan, was created in 1989 by centre-left dissidents from the PMDB. Like the toucan, the PSDB is top-heavy. It has big names but lacks votes and so, despite its more liberal ideology, it ended up adopting a neoliberal economic programme and allying with the conservative PFL in order to win the 1994 presidential election for President Fernando Henrique Cardoso.

**Partido Socialista Brasileiro** (PSB – Brazilian Socialist Party), presumably unlike any other socialist party, includes wealthy landowners among its members. It has become a party like any other, making alliances with left and right in order to gain power.

**Democratas** (Democrats) (ex-Partido da Frente Liberal [PFL – Liberal Front Party]), the party of the right wing, is strongest in rural states, and provides many of the congressmen in the *bancada ruralista*.

most parties have become agglomerations of politicians representing regional, class, corporate, business, or individual interests. The *ruralistas*, representing big farming and agribusiness, are one of the most powerful lobbies, with over 120 votes. The Amazon bloc brings together 90 mostly conservative, anti-environmental, anti-Indian congressmen and women from the nine Amazon states.

## Two Brazils

The constant changes masked an unchanging, unwritten political system based on patronage and privilege, which has only recently begun to crumble. The unofficial division of Brazilians into first- and second-class citizens is still visible in many regions and areas, most noticeably in the fact that slavery is still found, not only on remote Amazon ranches but in urban sweatshops. Nowadays dedicated teams of government inspectors hunt down the slave owners, many of whom are elected politicians. The names of the guilty people are published in a list each year, and they are denied credit from state banks. But the practice persists because it is more lucrative than obeying the law.

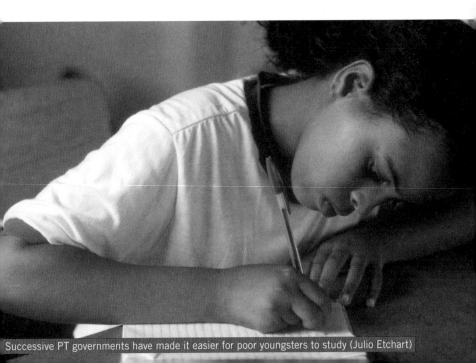

Successive PT governments have made it easier for poor youngsters to study (Julio Etchart)

The huge and very slowly diminishing gap between rich and poor has made the emergence of solid democratic institutions more difficult. Congress still remains unrepresentative, with few members defending the interests of the rural and urban poor, Afro-Brazilians, or indigenous communities, while hundreds of senators and deputies act together to prevent any real challenge to the property of landowners and the purses of the wealthy. Until the election as President of the PT's Luiz Inácio Lula da Silva in 2002, Brazil had never had a socialist or left-wing government. Even now, after Lula's two terms and Dilma's first, the need for a coalition to ensure a majority in congress has prevented any sweeping reforms.

## The reduction of poverty

The 12 years of PT governments, from 2002 until the present (2014), have nevertheless brought significant change for millions of poorer Brazilians, with a reduction in poverty, an increase in the minimum wage and a system of quotas and grants that has enabled hundreds of thousands of underprivileged young people to go to college or university. The upwardly mobile 'new middle classes', as they are called, now throng airports instead of bus terminals, shopping malls instead of street markets, and own cars and motorbikes.

More than 13 million families, most of them in the north-east, receive the Bolsa Família, a monthly allowance conditional upon sending children to school. It has revitalized the economy in many regions, and during the latest drought saved many families from having to leave their land. It has also drastically reduced the number of families joining land occupations organized by the MST (Landless Workers' Movement). The Bolsa Família is now said to be the largest income distribution programme in the world, and has become a model for many other countries.

The other major distribution programme, introduced in 2013 by the government of Dilma Rousseff, was Mais Médicos (More Doctors). The aim here was to encourage doctors to work in rural areas and poor city areas where there is a chronic shortage of doctors. Because many of the doctors who signed up came from Cuba, there was an outcry from Brazil's medical establishment, who tried to sabotage the programme.

## *Social movements*

The Movimento dos Trabalhadores Rurais Sem Terra (Landess Rural Workers' Movement, known as the MST or *sem terra*), is Brazil's largest and most innovative and successful social movement. With 60 agricultural co-operatives and 100 associations producing milk, beef, beans, maize, soya, manioc, fish and local fruits, the MST celebrated its 30th anniversary in 2014. A law introduced during Lula's presidency, obliging local authorities to buy 30 per cent of the fresh ingredients for school meals from small farmers, has given many settlements a guaranteed source of income.

For the MST the battle now is to counter the monocultures of agribusiness with an alternative model of mixed farming based on organic methods. 'Do we want monoculture farming that destroys the forests, requires huge amounts of pesticides and causes cancer, or one that produces healthy foods, generates jobs and preserves the environment?' asked MST spokesman Antônio Miranda.

Despite the MST's high hopes when Lula was elected, successive PT governments have created fewer and fewer new settlements for landless workers. Most of those that have been created are in the Amazon region, far from markets and infrastructure. At the same time, the number of those taking part in occupations to demand land – something that the MST used to be famous for

MST activists in a land occupation (Douglas Mansur/Arquivo MST)

– has fallen heavily. This has been put down to the success of the Bolsa Família programme, which means that poor families don't face the grinding, desperate poverty of the past.

## Protest movements of 2013

The mass protests that brought hundreds of thousands on to the streets in 2013 were originally sparked by a small group of activists calling themselves the Movimento Passe Livre (MPL – Free Pass Movement), which was campaigning for free bus transport in the main cities. When the municipal government of São Paulo announced a rise in bus fares in June, the group called a protest. It was small, but the police broke it up with unnecessary violence and, thanks to the abundance of smartphones, images of the confrontation went viral.

The result was an explosion of protests, with huge crowds, brought together by social media, complaining about everything anyone could think of: public transport, the education and health services, the government, political parties ('No Party Represents Me', said one banner), corruption and the spiralling cost of the football stadiums being built for the World Cup. ('FIFA standards in public service', said another banner). An anarchic fringe group called the Black Blocs vandalized banks and tried to invade public buildings. In Brasília the protesters tried to occupy ministries and the Congress building. To some extent the protests were effective. Under this popular pressure, senators and deputies acknowledged in their speeches the 'clamour of the streets', and worked far into the night to pass a record number of bills. Local authorities cancelled rises in bus fares.

But this burst of parliamentary activity lasted only a few days. By the end of 2013 the protests, which had spread all over Brazil, with sit-ins at town halls and road blocks, had also stopped, but it seems likely that they will flare up again, especially as most people feel that little has really changed.

## The Truth Commission

It took Brazil 28 years to set up its National Truth Commission, tasked with investigating crimes committed during the 21 years of military dictatorship, but without the authority to prosecute those accused of human rights crimes or even to oblige them to answer when questioned. The Commission has been given access to some – by no means all – of the archives of the dictatorship period. Its main focus is to discover what happened to the 400 or so disappeared political prisoners, including 60 members of a rural guerrilla movement who set up a base in the Amazon region of Araguaia in the early 1970s. They are also investigating the many crimes committed against indigenous peoples and rural workers, and the involvement of the diplomatic service in persecuting Brazilian exiles.

Additionally, many local truth commissions have been set up in universities, city halls and state legislatures. The National Truth Commission is due to report by December 2014, and it is expected to call for the repeal of the 1979 Amnesty Law, which has prevented any military or police officer being brought to trial for crimes of torture and murder.

## The political future

Whichever president is elected in the foreseeable future, it is likely that the so-called *bancada ruralista* – a large, powerful alliance of right-wing landowners and their allies – will continue to dominate Congress and to veto any attempt at more innovative or radical policies. This means that the huge dam-building programme in the Amazon, geared to producing cheap energy for aluminium companies and the rest of Brazil, will be carried forward, despite protests from indigenous and peasant communities, and that agri-business will continue to expand, despite attempts by the MST and others to curb it.

Yet change is coming. The 'new middle classes' go on expanding, while piling up credit-card debt. The widened access to further education and the growing numbers of young Brazilians studying abroad are building up a critical mass of more informed citizens. These are the people who will demand better services and less corruption, both via the social media and on the streets.

The days of families keeping entire states such as Maranhão and Alagoas in a feudal grip for decades are surely numbered. Brazil's progress from a deeply unequal society to a more egalitarian one still has a long way to go, but it has begun. The clock can no longer be turned back, as it was during the dark years of the military dictatorship, and it is ticking towards a better future. Brazil still is 'the land of the future', but that future is getting closer.

Many of the protesters in 2013 wear masks to hide their identity (Christian Tragni)

# 5 Society

Brazilian society is multiracial and complex, but remains hugely unequal more than 125 years after the end of slavery. While the country is a leading user of the internet and social media, Brazilians are shot dead in rural conflicts or because they live on the streets. Most of the population live in towns or cities, but small groups of isolated Indians still roam the Amazon forest.

## *Indians*

Place names like Guanabara, Curitiba, and Cuiabá are a perpetual reminder of Brazil's original inhabitants. Brazilians with not a drop of indigenous blood boast indigenous names like Iracema and Moacyr. Manioc flour and the *guaraná* drink are part of the national diet, and most fish, fruit, and fauna are known by their indigenous names.

Although more than 500 years of exposure to disease, violence and dispossession wiped out most Indians, in recent years there has been a marked increase in their numbers, with a rise of over 10 per cent between 2000 and 2010. Today, there are almost 900,000 Indians in Brazil in at least 238 indigenous groups, who live scattered across the country, but particularly in the Amazon, amounting to 0.4 per cent of the Brazilian population. Brazil's indigenous peoples speak 274 different languages, though 110 of these languages are spoken by fewer than 400 people. The term 'Indians' is of course technically incorrect; it owes its origin to the mistaken belief of the Europeans who reached Brazil that they had reached the mysterious East, which they indiscriminately called 'the Indies', but the term is still widely used in Brazil, even by indigenous people themselves.

Relations between the surviving indigenous groups and white society have fluctuated. During nationalist periods they have been romanticized as the most genuine of all Brazilians. In the 19th century this produced *Iracema*, a novel by José de Alencar that became a classic, and Brazil's only famous opera, *O Guarani*, by Carlos Gomes.

But in recent years Brazil's Indians have been under constant threat. Once the military regime began the drive to conquer the Amazon in the 1970s, they again came to be seen as obstacles to progress, development, and wealth. Roads were deliberately driven through reserves, spreading disease and introducing alcohol and prostitution. In 1974 the Indians began to fight back. Despite speaking different languages, they found that they had something in common: the need to stop their land being invaded.

The post-dictatorship Brazilian Constitution of 1988 guaranteed indigenous peoples' right to occupy their traditional territories, and as much land as they needed to maintain their way of life. But the indigenous peoples did not become the owners of their lands, which were held in trust for them by the state, and 'national interest' and 'national security' could override indigenous rights. According to the constitution, all indigenous land was to have been marked out – a process known as 'demarcation' – within five years, but 25 years after the constitution was promulgated fewer than half of Brazil's indigenous territories have been properly demarcated. The result has been constant invasions and land grabs, with the authorities generally looking the other way and doing little to prevent the collapse of indigenous communities, which they see as a barrier to 'development'.

Inoculation helps to improve the life of the Yanomami Indians (Fiona Watson/Survival International)

During the 1980s the threat to Brazil's indigenous peoples was symbolised by the situation of the Yanomami. Living in the north of the Amazon and numbering about 15,000, they are the last large group of relatively isolated Indians in the Americas. Another 12,000 live over the border in Venezuela. In their communal huts deep in the forest, most Yanomami still live a traditional existence, but in the 1980s thousands of *garimpeiros* (wildcat prospectors), supplied and supported by local businessmen and politicians, began invading their gold-rich territory. The result was the death of at least 1,500 Yanomami, who succumbed to malaria, TB, influenza, and malnutrition. Some were shot dead during clashes. Unable to find fish and game because of the noise and pollution of the gold miners' machinery, and abandoning their gardens because they were sometimes given sugar and rice by gold miners, many Yanomami starved.

Photographs of the disaster led to an international outcry, and the Yanomami territory was finally ratified as an indigenous reserve in 1992. Jungle airstrips were bombed from the air to try to prevent the *garimpeiros* returning. But when the price of gold goes up they always return. It is only after intense international pressure from NGOs like Survival International and the Yanomami's own organization, Hutukara, that the federal government leads operations to expel the gold miners, who still count on vociferous support from local politicians.

The demarcation of the neighbouring indigenous territory, Raposa Serra do Sol, which borders Venezuela and Guyana and is home to five indigenous peoples, was fiercely challenged by the local authorities and business interests, but finally signed into law in 2005, and confirmed by the Brazilian supreme court in 2009.

In 1996 a change in Indian land rights legislation permitted any person, company or local authority to lay claim to part of a reserve if they could come up with documents proving that it was theirs. A government memo admitted that the aim was to open the way for economic development 'in the areas where most indigenous peoples live' – the Amazon basin. The change was condemned by everyone, from the European Parliament to the Indians themselves, who said it would endanger their lives.

Now a further weakening of indigenous rights threatens as the PT government, listening to the demands of the rural lobby, plans to transfer authority over the land demarcation process from the Indian agency, FUNAI, to Congress. This is likely to put an end to further demarcation.

An eloquent example of what happens to tribes crowded into smaller and smaller reserves and forced to work in hostile surroundings comes from the Guaraní-Kaiowá people in Mato Grosso do Sul. Where they once occupied an area of forest and plains, they have gradually been squeezed into inadequate, over-crowded reservations to make way for cattle ranches and sugar-cane plantations for Brazil's biofuel industry. In the last 15 years the Guaraní-Kaiowá have organized and tried to take back their legitimate territory, but they have met armed resistance from ranchers, and several leaders, such as Marcos Veron, have been murdered.

In the Dourados reserve, for example, 12,000 Indians are living on little more than 3,000 hectares. The destruction of the forest has meant that hunting and fishing are no longer possible, and there is barely enough land even to plant crops. Malnutrition is a serious problem, and since 2005 at least 53 Guaraní children have died of starvation. Since 1986 517 Guaraní have committed suicide, most of them teenagers who worked in the local sugar-cane alcohol distilleries. The plight of the Guaraní-Kaiowá is the subject of the 2008 film *Birdwatchers*. The star of the film, Ambrósio Vilhalva, was murdered in 2013 after repeated threats.

Thrown off their traditional lands, Guarani Indians squat in roadside camps (Sarah Shenker/ Survival International)

FUNAI has a chequered history. Many FUNAI workers have been brave, dedicated people, some giving their lives to protect the Indians. But the agency has become associated with corruption, inefficiency, and a chronic lack of funds. Although FUNAI was set up as a guardian of indigenous interests, its officials have all too often conspired against the Indians in return for bribes from loggers, ranchers, and *garimpeiros*. Some Indian groups, too, have allowed loggers and *garimpeiros* on to their reserves in exchange for pitiable rewards of food, vehicles, or money.

Brazilian law, based on the positivist idea that one nation corresponds to one territory ruled by a single, monolithic state, does not accept the idea of a pluri-ethnic or multi-nation state. Successive governments have tried to integrate Indians into Brazilian society as individuals, which would effectively deny them any right to communal land or reserves. The Indians have an important ally, however: the Ministério Público Federal (MPF – Federal Public Ministry), an independent power, whose lawyers have the tasks of defending disadvantaged groups, particularly indigenous groups.

The Indians are fighting with growing sophistication for their right to be different. Their organizations, both national and regional, hold regular assemblies, organize protests and demonstrations, and increasingly collaborate with other popular movements such as the *sem terra* (landless peasants) who fight for land.

## Women

Although since 2011 Brazil has had its first-ever woman head of state, President Dilma Rousseff, until recently the only women mentioned in Brazilian history books were queens, princesses and mistresses. Women's rights have advanced since the 1988 constitution introduced equal rights and obligations for men and women, bringing Brazil into line with the most progressive European countries, but abortion is still a crime, except where rape can be proved. And a culture of *machismo* in many regions continues to encourage violence against women – Brazil's rate of violence against women is seventh-highest in the world, with at least 92,000 women killed in the last three decades. Last year President Dilma launched a project to build 'Casas da Mulher Brasileira' (Houses for the Brazilian Woman) in all state capitals, where women in need can find shelter and support.

Twenty per cent of households are now headed by women, and proportionally more women have paid jobs than in any other Latin American country. In the professions, Brazilian women are everywhere. More women than men graduate from university; two-thirds of medicine and journalism graduates and over half of the law graduates are women. Even in engineering, a traditionally male career, one-fifth of the graduates are now women. The supreme court currently has two women members and had a woman president in 2006–7, and it is estimated that around 30 per cent of judges are women, mainly in the lower courts.

Pay has yet to catch up, however. Women still earn, on average, three-quarters of men's pay for the same job, and the gap has been widening in recent years. In the state of São Paulo, Brazil's richest, the gap between men's and women's earnings is more than 30 per cent.

In politics, apart from the President herself, power remains firmly in male hands, with only a handful of women ministers, senators, and national deputies. A survey in 2013 by the Inter-Parliamentary Union into female representation in national

Dilma Rousseff was elected Brazil's first woman President in 2010 (Christian Tragni)

legislatures ranked Brazil 119th out of 142 countries, behind Pakistan and Afghanistan. One of the most prominent women in politics today is Marina Silva, a rubber-tapper's daughter from the Amazonian state of Acre, who learnt to read and write when she was 14 and went on to take a university degree. In 1994, at the age of 36, she became Brazil's youngest senator. Appointed environment minister in Lula's government in 2008, she later resigned in protest at the lack of support within government for environmental and climate policies, and left the PT.

The birth rate in Brazil has been falling steadily since the 1960s, and the decline has been particularly sharp since the 1980s. In 1980 a woman of childbearing age typically had four children, but by 2013 the figure had fallen to just under two. This means that, as in most developed countries, catholics are ignoring their church's official teaching on contraception. Information on contraceptive methods is widely available. Abortion is still a controversial issue, with fierce opposition to any relaxation in the law from the Catholic Church and some pentecostal churches. Nevertheless a million women a year have abortions in Brazil. Unsafe abortion is a problem for poorer women; those with resources can access safe procedures. Complications from illegal abortions are believed to be responsible for one-quarter of maternal deaths.

The falling birth rate, coupled with longer lives – the average life expectancy is now 74 – means that Brazil, still renowned for its youth culture, is in fact an ageing society. Almost 13 per cent of the population now is over 60.

## Children and adolescents

Brazilians believe that children should be seen and heard, even in restaurants late at night. Children from wealthier families are often pampered, waited on by maids, chauffeured by mothers to and from after-school activities. Children tend to grow up less inhibited in a society where touch is not taboo and affection is openly expressed. Brazilians like children, except when they live on the street; then they are perceived as a threat.

In 1990 Brazil passed a Children's Act that enshrined children's rights in law and introduced an innovative system of local children's councils. Yet violence against street children has continued; black teenagers living in slum areas are especially vulnerable to illegal police shootings or murder by death squads, often made up of off-duty policemen. In Brazil, the law and its practice are often distant relatives. A 2011 study put the number of children living on the streets of Brazil's biggest cities at just under 24,000; they usually end up there as a result of domestic violence and/or drug and alcohol abuse.

But life for children and young people as a whole in Brazil is improving, as almost all (98 per cent of 6–14-year-olds) attend school. In addition, 92 per cent of 5–6-year-olds now go to kindergarten and, at the other end of the age range, many more go on to higher education, aided by a government programme of grants, Pro-Uni.

Child labour ranges from children helping on a family farm to children sent out to earn money on the streets, with all the dangers that exposes them to. Official figures suggest that about half a million children still work but the number is falling rapidly. But the picture is very mixed across the country. In the centre-west, for instance, where cattle ranching and sugar-cane plantations are expanding, the number of working children is increasing rapidly.

Children help to harvest sisal (Julio Etchart)

## *Race and immigration*

Brazil's patron saint, Nossa Senhora da Aparecida, is a black Madonna, and more than half of Brazil's 201 million people are black or mixed race, but official Brazil is still overwhelmingly white. When a black parliamentary front was created in the late 1990s, it attracted only 12 of the 513 representatives. Recent governments have had a token number of black ministers, such as footballer Pelé as sports minister or singer/composer Gilberto Gil as minister of culture. Another notable exception is the current president of the supreme court, Joaquim Barbosa, who is black. Only recently have black people begun to play roles other than that of servants and criminals in television soap operas and adverts.

After descendants of Africans, people of European descent form the second-largest contingent. Following the original Portuguese colonists, hundreds of thousands of German and Italian immigrants settled in the south and south-east, and to this day you can find villages like Pomerode in Santa Catarina where German is still spoken. Blumenau's beer festival rivals Munich's, while São Paulo's pizzas yield nothing to Rome's. Dutch, Poles, Swiss, Finns, and American Confederates have all created their own enclaves. (The English do not have an enclave but they brought football!)

Japanese immigration began in 1906, when the first boatload of second sons arrived, unable to inherit land in their own overcrowded country. Many soon fled the harsh conditions of the coffee estates and headed for the cities, especially

Itinerant cinema for Japanese immigrants to Brazil in the 1930s (Saburo Yamanaka museum)

São Paulo, which now has three-quarters of a million first-, second-, and third-generation Japanese, making it the largest Japanese community outside Japan. They not only dominate the market gardening sector but have moved steadily up the social ladder. Yakotas, Uekis, Hanishoros, and Matsudas can be found in every area of business and politics. Wandering through São Paulo's Liberdade district, you might forget that you are in South America. All the shop signs are in Japanese (except for the occasional Chinese or Korean restaurant) and there are stores crammed with Japanese foodstuffs and locally produced Japanese newspapers.

In the 1980s, Japanese immigration went into reverse as thousands of descendants of Japanese immigrants left for Japan in search of a better life. They were disappointed to find that, although they looked Japanese and might even speak the language, they were still treated as foreigners – their Brazilian lack of formality instantly gave them away.

Brazil has also seen an influx of Lebanese and Palestinians since the 1970s, adding to its older Arab colony of Egyptians and Syrians. In the interior, where many Arabs used to work as travelling salesmen, they are confusingly called *turcos* (Turks). Like the Jewish community, the Arabs have founded hospitals and clubs, and the two communities have been able to work together. Not so long ago, the president of the São Paulo stock market was an Arab, and his vice-president a Jew.

A casual visitor from Britain, looking at the mix of colours and ethnic types, and the number of interracial couples, might wonder why Brazil did not claim the title of 'rainbow nation' long before South Africa. The answer has to do with slavery and the way it was abolished. Brazil was the last country in the Americas to abolish slavery, in 1888, but nothing was done to integrate or improve the lot of the former slaves, so that they merely remained a layer at the bottom of Brazilian society. At the same time governments promoted immigration from Europe with an explicit policy of 'whitening' the nation. The military dictators of the 1960s and 1970s promoted the myth of 'racial democracy'. Even the PT failed to set up a group to study racism until 1995.

Over the centuries there was resistance from the black communities. Slaves maintained their ancestral religions in the back yards of the slave houses, with the result that *candomblé* and similar forms of religion are thriving today. Runaway slaves also founded free communities, or *quilombos*, in remote areas (see Chapter 3). But the modern assertive black movement goes back no further than 1978. The first law against racial discrimination in Brazil was introduced in 1951, and penalties were considerably increased by a law of 1989. Nevertheless, Afro-Brazilians are still likely to be poorer and less well-educated than those from other ethnic groups.

In 2012 a law was introduced obliging federal universities to keep half their places for students from state schools, and a similar quota for non-white students who meet entrance requirements, in accordance with the racial mix of the state in which the university is located. The quota is being introduced gradually.

Continuing racial discrimination was highlighted at the beginning of 2014 when young, mainly black, people from deprived areas organized a series of 'spins round the shopping malls', known as *rolezinhos*. They organized mass tours of exclusive shopping malls from which they would normally have been excluded. These mainly non-violent protests led to the closure of some malls. The final feature of life for many poor black men in Brazil is early death. A study published in 2011, with the significant title *The Colour of Murder*, found that while murders of young white men fell by a quarter between 2001 and 2010, murders of young black men increased by almost 36 per cent.

## Religion

The name of God is on everyone's lips in Brazil because of the ubiquitous catchphrase *'se Deus quiser'*, 'God willing'. 'Inflation will be lower this month, God willing', says every minister of finance. *'Se Deus quiser*, I will get that bandit', swears the policeman, cradling his machine-gun. Few Brazilians would admit to being atheist, but their relations with God tend to be practical rather than spiritual. Long-distance trucks sport hand-painted slogans invoking divine protection.

Churches like the Basilica of Our Lady of Aparecida, near São Paulo, are crammed with *ex-votos* – plaster casts of legs, hands, torsos, heads, whichever body part was cured by divine intervention. On saints' days the roads are clogged with buses and trucks full of pilgrims going to 'pay their promises' – give thanks for mercies received. One reason for this is the way that Christianity, in the form of Roman Catholicism, came to Brazil in the 16th century. Relatively few clergy came with the invaders, and the result was that the religion that was established over much of the country was a version of popular pre-reformation Portuguese catholicism, with all its folklore and superstition.

Roman Catholicism remained a conservative force until the middle of the 20th century: on the day of the military coup in 1964, the bishops' conference gave thanks for Brazil's delivery from communism. But, as the repressive nature of the military regime became apparent, the bishops issued ever-stronger statements criticizing torture, censorship, social injustice, and the lack of land reform, and calling for a return to Christianity. A key figure in the renewal of the Catholic Church in Brazil was the archbishop of Recife, Helder Câmara, who created the central administrative structure of the church, the bishops' conference, which had a secretariat with departments for social as well as religious issues; these included CIMI, the Indigenist Missionary Council, set up in 1972, and CPT, the Pastoral Land Commission, founded in 1975, to support and campaign for the Indians and landless peasants threatened by invasions, evictions, and violence.

The archbishop of Brazil's biggest city and business capital, São Paulo, Cardinal Paulo Evaristo Arns, was also a radical. Arns made his church a centre of resistance to the military regime. There, he received and comforted the mothers of disappeared prisoners, wives of imprisoned strikers, peasants who had been tortured, and refugees from other Latin American regimes. He was also sought out by multinational executives, military emissaries, and even, once or twice, by repentant torturers. When Jewish journalist Vladimir Herzog died as a result of torture – announced as suicide – Arns organized an ecumenical service which became an act of defiance towards the regime and the police and troops who had encircled the cathedral. As a result of this new social commitment, churchmen and women, such as the US religious Dorothy Stang, murdered in Pará in February 2005, became targets themselves.

As reform in the Catholic Church gained ground throughout Latin America, priests and nuns began to leave comfortable city-centre parishes and establish communities in the rapidly growing shanty towns. Part of this effort to take the church out of its comfort zone was the formation of church base communities (*comunidades eclesiais de base*), groups of believers who met to discuss the implications of their faith for the injustices they experienced in their everyday lives. They spread rapidly all over Brazil, aided by the shortage of priests, which made the idea of laity-led groups more attractive to the church. At their peak, they numbered 80,000 separate groups. During the military dictatorship the Catholic Church provided sanctuary for the opposition movement – the only voice left for those without a voice and often the only place where trade unionists and human rights activists could meet in safety. The base communities were one of the factors in the formation of the new Workers' Party, the PT.

In 1979 the election of the Polish cardinal Karol Wojtyla as Pope John-Paul II gave the conservatives their chance to fight back. A staunch anti-communist, he was easily persuaded that the 'option for the poor' and liberation theology were a Marxist infiltration of the church. Bishops like Arns were out of favour. The leading Brazilian exponent of liberation theology, Leonardo Boff, was harassed. However, radical commitment did not disappear completely, as CIMI and the CPT defended indigenous people and poor farmers who were facing the onslaught of agribusiness and hydroelectric schemes.

Pentecostal worshippers (Christian Tragni)

Change eventually came. By the time the base communities met for their thirteenth assembly in January 2014, they received a message of greeting from Pope Francis – the first time a Pope had ever communicated with the meeting. For the Catholic Church in Brazil as a national institution, however, it may be too late. Between 1980 and 2010 the number of catholics in Brazil fell by a quarter, as protestant, and especially pentecostal, churches increased their membership.

Traditional protestant churches, Anglicans, Methodists, Presbyterians and Baptists, gradually became established in Brazil during the 19th century, but in the 1980s and 1990s a new sort of protestantism took Brazil by storm. The pentecostals had arrived. Typically the pentecostal churches sprang up in converted cinemas and bingo halls across the country. Between 1990 and 1992, 710 new churches, about five a week, were opened in Rio, 90 per cent of them pentecostal. During the same period only one new catholic church was consecrated.

The first of these new-style churches was the Igreja Universal do Reino de Deus (Universal Church of the Kingdom of God), led by self-styled Bishop Edir Macedo, a former lottery clerk. In the days of high inflation, smartly dressed ushers raced up and down the aisles collecting sack-loads of money as worshippers dutifully paid their tithes. Preachers told them that giving was the way to godliness. At the end of 1995, the church was being investigated for fraud and charlatanism after a former preacher revealed the dubious methods used to extract more money from worshippers. Macedo has become a wealthy man, owning a fast-growing TV network and scores of radio stations. He is spreading his empire to many other countries in Latin America, Africa, Europe, and the USA. More recently another charismatic leader, Silas Malafaia, leader of the Assembleia de Deus Vitória em Cristo (Assembly of God Victory in Christ), has become a national figure, among other things notable for his homophobic utterances. His church appeals to the newly prosperous lower middle class, and in 2011 he was being courted by the main national TV network, Globo. Pentecostals are also making their presence felt in Congress. The best-known example is the pastor Marco Feliciano, who, despite his notorious homophobic remarks, was elected as chair of the human rights committee of the lower house of Congress.

The success of the pentecostals has been a topic for anxious discussion among catholics over the last 25 years. Among the factors for their success is that they offer an attractive mix of emotion, participation, and faith healing. Their simplistic, fundamentalist interpretation of the bible offers a clear moral code and a sense of self-respect, and the emphasis of some churches on prosperity as a sign of divine favour has matched the aspirations of those who aimed to leave poverty behind in the consumer boom of the early 21st century. Pentecostal churches have a more flexible structure: their pastors do not need to be celibate or male – though most are male – nor do they need six years of academic training. As a result, they tend to come from the same class and culture as their congregations, unlike the priests of the Catholic Church, who may have started poor but have been educated into a sort of intellectual elite.

The African slaves brought their own gods with them, but as open worship was banned, they disguised them with catholic names. So Ogum became St George, Iansa became St Barbara. The hybrid religions thrive today under their own names, *candomblé*, *macumba*, and *umbanda*. Candles burning at a crossroads or the headless body of a black hen are signs of a *trabalho*, an offering to the gods for something desired, or a curse on somebody. Whatever their religion, most Brazilians will treat such signs with respect.

In Bahia, which has Brazil's largest black population, *candomblé* priestesses have become well-known personalities, respected by political leaders. Syncretic practices, like the ceremony of washing the steps of the church of Nosso Senhor do Bonfim by *candomblé* followers, have become a regular tradition. On New Year's Eve, a million people of all religions pack the beaches of Rio to throw offerings into the sea for the goddess Iemanjá. Brazilians find no problem in keeping a foot in more than one church, selecting what they like from each religion.

## Gay life in Brazil

The Portuguese state used Brazil as a dumping ground for 'social misfits', which included homosexuals. The lives of homosexuals in colonial Brazil are vividly described in João Trevisan's book *Devassos no Paraíso* (*Perverts in Paradise*). Independent Brazil, however, had no legislation against homosexual activity. The gay movement in Brazil began with the group Somos in São Paulo in the 1970s and the newspaper *Lampião*, produced in Rio de

Janeiro. One of the most important gay groups, the Grupo Gay da Bahia, was founded in 1980, and campaigned for the removal of homosexuality from the official list of diseases. As in other countries, the AIDS crisis stimulated the growth of gay self-help groups, which also campaigned for gay and lesbian rights at a time when the disease was commonly described as the 'gay plague'. In the 1990s national organizations for lesbians and transsexuals were formed, and in 1995 the Associação Brasileira de Lésbicas, Gays, Bissexuais, Travestis e Transexuais (ABGLT – Brazilian Association of Gays, Lesbians, Transvestites and Transsexuals), the first network representing the range of diversity among lesbians, gays and transgendered people, was founded. The first Gay Pride march was held in São Paulo in 1997, and it is now said to be the biggest tourist attraction in Brazil after the Rio carnival.

Despite a vibrant LGBT culture in many parts of Brazil, hate crime against LGBT people is still a serious problem: the Gay Group of Bahia recorded 338 homophobic murders in 2012, an increase of over a quarter since 2011. Brazil has no national legislation outlawing homophobia. Attempts to make homophobia a federal crime were blocked in Brazil's senate in December 2013 by the 'evangelical bloc', with support from conservative catholics. The abandonment of the legislation was celebrated on Twitter by Pastor Silas Malafaia, who described its supporters as a 'band of devils'. Since 2004 the federal government has had a programme

Gay parade in São Paulo (Christian Tragni)

titled Brazil without Homophobia, but in 2011 President Dilma Rousseff cancelled the distribution to state schools of an educational pack on sexual orientation after pressure from conservative religious groups.

More positively, following a ruling in 2011 from the federal supreme court that extended marriage to persons of the same gender, the judiciary decreed in 2013 that it was unlawful for the authorities to refuse to marry people of the same gender. And – just to show how conservative the mainstream media are – the first gay kiss in a Brazilian soap had to wait until January 2014.

## Health

Health standards in Brazil are improving, especially in maternal and infant mortality, but deficiencies in the state health service are responsible for serious problems, such as the rise in the number of deaths of women from breast cancer. Brazil has had a public universal health system, the Sistema Único de Saúde (SUS), since 1998, but it is widely criticized for delay and poor services. With the increasing affluence in the 21st century, the number of people taking out private health insurance has almost doubled, but the services offered by private companies have not kept pace with this growth, though their income has quadrupled since 2001. Brazil is not in fact short of doctors – it has double the World Health Organization's recommended ratio of doctors to population – but they tend to be in affluent areas, and not in remote rural communities.

## Drugs

'Crackland' in the centre of São Paulo, an area where crack users have occupied abandoned buildings and openly use crack, hit the headlines in early 2012, when the drugs squad, under the authority of the state government, launched an assault on the area, code-named 'Pain and Suffering'. In 2014 the recently elected PT mayor, Fernando Haddad, launched a programme known as Open Arms, designed to wean addicts from their dependence by providing them with hostels and paid employment such as street cleaning.

According to the 2013 UN World Drug Report, cocaine consumption in Brazil is increasing, whereas in the rest of South America it is falling, and Brazil is ranked second after the USA in world cocaine consumption. A random test of drivers in Brazil in 2011 found that 39 per cent had traces of cocaine in their blood, and 32 per cent cannabis. Brazil is also an important route for cocaine trafficking, partly because it has a 10,000-mile border, largely in jungle, with the main producer countries, Bolivia, Peru and Colombia, and a long Atlantic coastline dotted with airports and ports. Its long land border with Paraguay, a big marijuana producer, makes smuggling this drug easy. It is too early to say how the decision of Uruguay, another neighbour with a land border, to embark on a controlled experiment of allowing marijuana to be grown and consumed, will affect Brazil.

## Prisons

Brazil has the world's fourth-largest prison population, with just under half a million people incarcerated. According to the United Nation's Subcommittee on the Prevention of Torture, torture is widespread and systematic, along with 'endemic overcrowding, filthy conditions of confinement, extreme heat, light deprivation and permanent lock-ups'.

Brazil's largest criminal organization is the Primeiro Comando da Capital (PCC – First Command of the Capital). Begun in São Paulo after a police massacre in Carandiru prison in 1992, which led to at least 111 deaths, it is believed to control 135 out of Brazil's 152 prisons and have some 20,000 members, about half of whom are in jail. Because of lax security, they control criminal activities from the prison using mobile phones, and are believed to monopolize drug-trafficking in the state of São Paulo.

In the run-up to the 2014 World Cup, a new police unit, called the Unidade de Polícia Pacificadora (UPP – Pacifying Police Unit), drove out drug leaders from central *favelas* near the richer areas of the city. Although it led to a decline in crime in these *favelas*, and its actions were broadly welcomed, it was controversial, as traffickers fled to more distant *favelas*, and these have become more dangerous places to live in.

## Violence

The 2013 edition of Brazil's annual study of violent deaths, *A Mapa da Violência,* notes that from the 1990s murders in Brazil began to outrank traffic accidents as the main cause of death.

Between 2008 and 2011 there were just over 206,000 murders in Brazil, 27.4 per 100,000 people. Brazil had the seventh-highest murder rate in the world in 2011. In the decade 2001–11, the murder rate of women increased twice as fast as that of men. Young people, particularly young black men, are dying at a horrific rate: in 2011 in Maceió, the state capital of Alagoas, the rate was a horrifying 288.1 murders per 100,000 young people. Eight other state capitals – Salvador, Vitória, Recife, Fortaleza, Natal, Manaus, Belém and Belo Horizonte – had youth murder rates of more than 100 per 100,000.

According to a joint report from Fórum Brasileiro de Segurança Pública (Brazil's Forum of Public Security) and the US non-governmental organization Open Society Foundations, 1890 people were killed by police in 23 Brazilian states in 2012, an average of five per day. As 89 police were killed while on duty, this means that 21 civilians died for the death of every police officer. The Forum pointed out that in the United States, with a population 60 per cent larger than Brazil's and with more fire-arms in circulation, 410 civilians were killed during the same year. Police death squads, set up during the military dictatorship to combat 'subversives', are also still active.

Woman smoking crack in São Paulo street (Christian Tragni)

Drilling for oil in the Campos Basin (Sue Cunningham)

# 6 The Economy

For more than a decade Brazil has (alphabetically at least) led the BRICS group of emerging economies – Brazil, Russia, India, China, and South Africa. Although the economy has not grown as rapidly as many had hoped, the country has won international acclaim for its anti-poverty programmes, which have lifted half the population out of poverty, and recent years have seen a consumer boom among the emerging poor, which has led to shortages of white goods like refrigerators. In the second decade of the 21st century this success received international recognition. With the 2014 World Cup and the 2016 Olympics, the world flocks to this South American giant to share its place in the sun.

Unfortunately, not all Brazilians have welcomed the international celebration. As has been discussed elsewhere (see Chapter 4), the heavy outlay on the stadiums turned the spotlight on shortcomings in the public services provided by the state. 'We want FIFA-quality hospitals', shouted the demonstrators in 2013. These demands were being made just as Brazil's economy began to slow down and the government's recent solution of throwing just enough money at potential social problems to dampen them down was no longer available. Moreover, the public was becoming fearful that recent economic success might prove another flash in the pan, as has happened so many times in the past.

## Boom and bust

'Everything that is planted here grows', Pedro Alvares Cabral wrote home ecstatically in 1500. Brazil's role, as in other European colonies, was to be plundered for the enrichment of the mother country. At different times in the ensuing 500 years, Brazilian products dominated world trade, providing the raw materials, such as sugar, coffee, rubber, and gold, that became essential to the way of life of the developed world.

During the gold boom in the 17th century, Brazilians (excluding the slaves) had the highest per capita income in the world. Brazil has always been a rich country, but its wealth has remained in the hands of the few. Little has been shared with those who helped to create it.

The first Brazilian export, the redwood used to make a dye much in demand in Europe, set the pattern. For 30 years after the arrival of the colonizers, 300 tons a year were exported until the accessible wood was exhausted and trade declined. Since 2001 the logging, sale and export of mahogany has been banned in Brazil to prevent its complete extinction.

## Sugar and gold

For 400 years the Brazilian economy was dominated by successive single product cycles of boom and bust. After redwood came sugar, its master-and-slave system leaving a legacy that still shapes Brazilian society today. 'King Sugar' produced over half of all export earnings during the entire colonial period. Then came gold. Such was the exitement that the Portuguese had to pass legislation to stop the Portuguese from emigrating en masse.

In the 17th century, Brazil was the world's greatest gold producer, and the capital city moved south from Salvador, near the sugar-cane fields of the north-east, to Rio de Janeiro, close to the gold mines of Minas Gerais. Brazil became the engine of Portugal's economy, its gold paying for imports of British manufactured goods. In this way, Brazilian gold helped to finance Britain's industrial revolution, but in Brazil itself the Portuguese monarchy banned industrial development, so that all available manpower would be available for agriculture and mining.

## Coffee

After sugar and gold came coffee. Coffee may seem as Brazilian as football and carnival, but it is an imported plant, first brought to Brazil from French Guiana in 1727 by a certain Sergeant Palheta. The climate and soil in the south, around Rio, São Paulo and, much later, Paraná, proved ideal for coffee. By the 1900s, Brazil was the world's major producer; coffee remained its leading export from 1831 to 1973. Immigrants rapidly replaced slaves on the coffee plantations – in one 20-year period, from 1879 to 1899, nearly one million immigrants settled in São Paulo state.

Whereas sugar had concentrated wealth in a few hands, coffee helped to spread it. Coffee, unlike sugar, could be grown by smallholders. Neither was it a monopoly crop: beans and cereals could be grown between the rows of bushes. Coffee brought development: railways and ports had to be built to transport it to overseas consumer markets. Santos, on the São Paulo coast, is still Brazil's biggest port, though now it exports cars and machinery as well as coffee and fruit. Coffee wealth paid for elegant country houses furnished with the best that Europe had to offer. Large mansions began to appear in what was the small provincial town of São Paulo, and the city became Brazil's main financial centre. Money brought industry and political power in its wake.

At the end of the 19th century came the shortest of all Brazil's commodity cycles, rubber. The USA and Europe clamoured for rubber to make tyres. Manaus briefly became the wealthiest city in Brazil as fortunes were made from the latex collected by enslaved Indians. But plantation rubber from Malaya and Ceylon swamped the market, and Brazilian rubber's share of the world trade fell from 90 per cent in 1910 to 2 per cent in 1937 (See Chapter 3).

Coffee spread out to dry in the sun in Rio de Janeiro state (Sue Cunningham)

Before and after independence, the British had dominated Brazil and other Latin American economies, finding them doubly useful as suppliers of essential raw materials and markets for the products of the mills and factories that mushroomed with Britain's industrial revolution. But by the Second World War, the USA had replaced Britain as Brazil's dominant trading partner, supplying 50 per cent of its imports and taking 40 per cent of its exports.

## Industrialization

In the 1940s, President Getúlio Vargas laid the foundations of Brazil's post-war industrial boom by creating giant state steel and oil companies and nationalizing Brazil's 20 private railways. Between 1950 and 1980, first under elected governments and then under military rule, Brazil's economy enjoyed an average annual growth rate of 7 per cent, one of the longest periods of sustained high growth in world history. In a far cry from today's free market economics, the government subsidized and directed private-sector activity, whether local or foreign.

State-led industrialization and import substitution led to rapid urbanization. Within 30 years Brazil was transformed from a largely rural society into a country where three-quarters of the

Workers still face overcrowded trains but they no longer travel on the roof as they did in the late 20th century (Julio Etchart)

population lived in towns and cities. A large workforce was needed for the new factories being set up by companies from Europe and the USA, attracted by tax incentives of all sorts, to produce cars, TV sets, and domestic appliances. Even so, job supply failed to keep up with demand, as millions of impoverished peasants flocked to the cities in search of new jobs. Corporations dominated the private sector, producing consumer goods, while the military concentrated on developing their own missiles, planes, armoured cars, and weapons, swiftly turning Brazil into a major arms exporter.

### Rising debts

Foreign loans poured into Brazil as Western bankers rushed to off-load their surplus dollars, regardless of the long-term viability of the projects they were financing. Whether they went to state or to private companies, these loans were made at floating interest rates, and their repayment was guaranteed by the government. Foreign debt was nothing new. At independence in 1822, Brazil already owed more than £3 million to London banks. The Brazilian economic miracle of the 1970s was loquaciously admired by First World bankers and politicians (who preferred to remain silent about the torture, censorship, and repression being exposed by human rights organizations).

The Itaipu dam, one of the largest hydroelectric power stations in the world, began operations in 1984
(Sue Cunningham)

Brazil's 'miracle' was finally destroyed by the military's disastrous response to the oil shocks of the 1970s. The steep rise in oil prices meant that Brazil, an oil importer, was suddenly faced with a greatly increased oil bill and a resulting trade deficit. Unwilling to admit the country's difficulties, President Ernesto Geisel, the fourth general to run the country since the 1964 coup, reacted with imperial disdain. Brazil, he declared, was an island of tranquillity, and recession was unnecessary. Instead Brazil simply borrowed more dollars to cover the trade deficit, adding to the debt being run up by such bodies as Eletrobrás, the state energy utility, and the other state companies involved in the military's ambitious programme of nuclear power stations, giant dams, roads, railways and a petrochemical complex.

## *Enter the IMF*

Crisis turned into disaster when the second oil shock of 1979 was followed by a dramatic rise in US interest rates. Brazil teetered on the edge of default. Between 1983 and 1985 it submitted seven letters of intent to the International Monetary Fund (IMF), agreeing to free-market reforms in return for a partial debt bailout. The government imposed savage cuts in social spending, inflicting a huge cost on ordinary Brazilians. Economic stagnation followed as Brazil added dollars to its long list of exports to the First World. By 1985, when the 21-year-long military regime finally handed power to a civilian government, inflation was on the rise and the country was in the worst recession since the depression of the 1920s.

Once the generals had gone, strikes for higher wages took off, and inflation spiralled to nearly 20 per cent per month. Between 1985 and 1994 there were three economic reform policies and four changes of currency, but nothing seemed to work. The most drastic measure was taken by President Collor, when he sequestered bank savings (see Chapter 3). His successor, Itamar Franco, continued to privatize and open up the economy to foreign ownership.

## *The* real

In 1993 Franco's finance minister, Fernando Henrique Cardoso, designed with his team of advisers a new stabilization programme.

The plan involved the biggest currency switch ever carried out in any country: a new currency, the *real*, loosely pegged to the US dollar, replaced the *cruzeiro*, and billions of banknotes and coins were distributed throughout the country. The *real* remains Brazil's currency today.

The impact of the *real* was dramatic: inflation fell from 40 per cent in June 1994 to 1 per cent in September, bringing immediate relief to wage-earners, whose wages now maintained their value instead of being halved each month. The end to the nightmare of galloping inflation ensured the election of Cardoso as President in October 1994, for the first of two terms. In 1996 concern began to grow as industry was undercut by cheap imports, unemployment soared and the economy was battered by some of the highest interest rates in the world, as the government sought to attract foreign capital into the country to service the huge public debt.

As the 2002 presidential election campaign reached its climax and Luiz Inácio Lula da Silva, the PT candidate, appeared poised for victory, foreign bankers began to panic at the prospect a 'leftist' government. In response, Lula published an open *Letter to the Brazilian People* (but with an eye to foreign investors) promising to stick to conservative economic policies. As President

President Fernando Henrique Cardoso (Sue Cunningham)

he kept his word, and in his first term of office kept public spending under tighter control than Cardoso. But one important difference from Cardoso was the policy of real increases in the minimum wage – the basis for calculating wages in much of the economy. The minimum wage increased in real terms by 72 per cent between 2002 and 2014.

Another important policy of the PT government was to build on the conditional family allowance introduced by Cardoso. This internationally lauded *Bolsa Família* programme is paid to mothers in poor families on condition that their children stay in school up to the age of 15 and have regular health checks. In 2013 13.8 million families, or almost 50 million people, were receiving this and related benefits, receiving on average R$216 (£55) a month. This package of benefits is believed to have reduced infant mortality and improved educational perfor-mance. One problem, however, is that the quality of state educa-tion and health services is in general quite low.

During his first term of office (2003–07) Lula benefited from a buoyant world economy and high prices for Brazil's exports such as minerals, crude oil, and soya. When the 2008 recession hit, and the São Paulo stock exchange lost more than 7 per cent of its value in one day, the government's social spending helped Brazil to avoid recession. In 2006 the government had launched the Programa de Aceleração do Crescimento (PAC – Accelerated Growth Programme) to remedy Brazil's notoriously inadequate infrastructure in roads, harbours and housing. This was badly needed, as investment in infrastructure had fallen by two-thirds

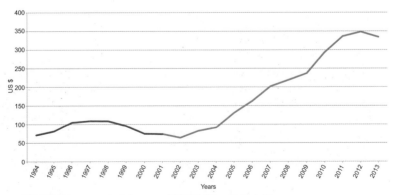

Source: Portal Brasil

between 1970 and 2000. The PAC doubled public investment in infrastructure over five years and is credited with creating 8.2 million jobs.

The increased income channelled to some of the poorest people in Brazilian society created a consumer boom. Forty-two million people opened their first bank accounts during Lula's presidency, and 15 million made their first trip by plane. The World Bank put numbers to the improvement. The proportion of Brazilians living in poverty fell from 21 per cent in 2003 to 11 per cent in 2009, and the proportion living in extreme poverty fell from 10 per cent in 2004 to 2.2 per cent in 2009. Perhaps more significantly, in roughly the same period the poorest 10 per cent of the population increased their incomes by 7 per cent, while the richest 10 per cent increased theirs by 1.7 per cent. There is still a long way to go, however: in 2012 just over half of Brazilian homes had a washing machine, 42 per cent had a car and 46 per cent had a computer with internet access. Only 57 per cent of homes were connected to a sewerage system.

Increased prosperity, though, is a two-edged sword in a country where basic services are so poor. As people have more money to spend, they want to escape the precarious education and health services provided by the state, but can't afford to buy these services from the private sector. The trade union research centre DIEESE argued at the end of 2013 that the necessary minimum wage for a family to have a decent standard of living was four times its actual level, fixed for 2014 at R$724 (£188) per month. The frustration felt by the poor, even those whose standard of living has been rising, helps to explain the protests that exploded in mid-2013.

## *Concreting the Amazon*

If investment in social infrastructure that benefits the mass of Brazilians has been neglected, one area where projects have been pushed forward is the construction of a series of dams to meet Brazil's increasing energy needs. With most of the hydroelectric potential in the rest of the country already tapped, the government now plans for hydro-power in the future to come from the ecologically sensitive Amazon region. These mega-projects are to be financed by Brazil's development bank, the BNDES, which provides heavily subsidized loans to construction companies, mainly the country's five largest – Norberto Odebrecht, Andrade Gutierrez, OAS, Queiroz Galvão and Camargo Corrêa. As a result, the Amazon economy is growing fast, but thousands of peasant hamlets and indigenous communities are facing the destruction of their way of life.

## Business and politics

The BNDES's close relationship with a few extremely large Brazilian companies is a good illustration of the links between politicians and business, especially since the privatization programme began in the 1990s. Particularly striking is the web of interests in the Brazilian Congress around the key sectors of mining and energy, through commissions overseeing the ministry of mines and energy and its department of mineral production. Through membership of these bodies, politicians are able to get friends and allies appointed to key positions in the ministry. Most of these politicians are members of the PMDB, the party that ruled after the military dictatorship and guaranteed the military impunity for their crimes.

At the centre of the web is ex-President José Sarney. He and his family are often described as exercising feudal control over their

The cable cars in Rio de Janeiro were funded by PAC (Christian Tragni)

home state of Maranhão: his daughter Roseanna is in her second term as state governor. One of José Sarney's associates, Edison Lobão, currently minister of mines and energy, increased his wealth from R$1.66 million (£400,000) in 2001 to R$5.9 million (£1.5m) in 2010. His good fortune, however, is modest compared with that of a former politician, Antônio da Justa Feijão, who is now superintendent of the mining department in the state of Amapá, Brazil's smallest state, for which Sarney is, incidentally, senator. Feijão's assets increased 240-fold between 2000 and 2010, from R$22,000 (£6,000) to R$5.63 million (£1.4 million).

## *Brazilian business abroad*

BNDES's statutes were changed in 2003 to allow the bank to finance activities by Brazilian companies abroad. Since then it has opened offices in Montevideo, London and Johannesburg, with Lula on record as saying that he wanted the bank to be 'ten times bigger than the World Bank'. According to the non-governmental organization Instituto Brasileiro de Análises Sociais e Econômicas (IBASE – Brazilian Institute of Social and Economic Analysis), between 1998 and 2013 BNDES invested in 48 projects being undertaken by Brazilian companies in other parts of Latin America. Twenty-six of these projects were operated by one company, Norberto Odebrecht SA. In contracts with foreign governments, BNDES stipulates that Brazilian companies must be employed in these projects.

Several such projects are part of a programme known as Initiative for the Integration of the Regional Infrastructure of South America (IIRSA). Among its projects is the 'Transoceanic Highway', a road driven from the western Brazilian state of Acre through Peru's Amazon region to its Pacific ports. The purpose of this highway is to speed the export of lucrative Brazilian exports to Pacific markets, notably China. Since 2007 BNDES has also released several million dollars for projects in Africa, in countries such as Angola, Mozambique, Ghana, South Africa and Equatorial Guinea and, when in office, President Lula actively promoted these economic links. The Bank has been described as operating like the World Bank 20 years ago, with very little transparency, inadequate consultation with local communities and inadequate regard for environmental impact.

In 2007 the state oil company, Petrobrás, announced the discovery of vast off-shore oil fields, enough to turn Brazil into a major energy player. At the time President Lula commented euphorically that the country had 'won the world lottery'. By 2014, however, prospects appeared more modest. Foreign multinationals, strongly attracted to tar sands in Canada and fracking in the USA, had not poured investment into Brazil, where access to this new oil, buried deep at sea, is technologically challenging and very expensive. Even so, in early 2014 Petrobrás officials were still talking about exporting 1.6 million barrels of oil a day by 2020, well down on earlier predictions but still an ambitious goal – as much as Venezuela is currently exporting. Some international experts remain sceptical.

## *Flaws appear*

Brazil ended 2013 with economic growth bumping along the bottom, with predictable calls for cuts in social spending and a curbing of increases in the minimum wage. In response, PT politicians have been repeating Lula's claim made during the 2010 election campaign: 'We have proved that looking after the poor is cheap.' As far as the *Bolsa Família* is concerned, this is certainly true. It costs only 0.4 per cent of GDP, less than a quarter of similar programmes in Europe and the US, but it boosts consumer spending by 1.78 per cent, since the poor tend not to save, but to buy more, particularly more food and more household goods.

Yet criticisms can be made of the economic strategy developed first by Cardoso and then continued and modified by the PT governments. Perhaps the most serious problem with current economic policies is that they are turning the country, which was becoming an industrial power, back into an exporter of primary goods, that is, products with no added value, such as minerals and unprocessed agricultural produce. According to the government's Instituto de Pesquisa Econômica Aplicada (IPEA – Institute of Applied Economic Research), the share of manufactured goods in Brazil's exports fell from 55 per cent in 2005 to 36 per cent in 2011, while the share of primary products rose from 29 per cent to 48 per cent in the same period. This is such a marked change that many economists talk of Brazil's 'deindustrialization', somewhat similar to the process that the UK economy has experienced over the last 30 years, though less extreme.

Some government officials shake off these criticisms, maintaining that Brazil, with its vast natural resources and abundant farmland, can forge a new path to development. Agribusiness has firmly established itself as the mainstay of the economy, they say, and, with the world fast running out of new land to cultivate, this is a trump card. Yet many development economists are sceptical that Brazil will be able to reach the level of development that the population yearns for while remaining heavily reliant on the export of primary products, the price of which is notoriously fickle. The country would do far better, they say, to follow the example of South Korea: seek to develop sophisticated industrial technology so that it can boost exports of manufactured goods, which guarantee a much more secure long-term income. Despite the lip service paid by the government to supporting manufacturing, however, much of Brazilian industry remains in the doldrums, some isolated successes notwithstanding. The accountants Deloitte identified poor infrastructure and a poor education system as the main reasons for this disappointing performance; it is interesting to note that one of the chief demands made by the June 2013 protesters was for much greater investment by the government in education.

This is likely to remain a point of conflict in future years. Those who took to the streets in 2013 were not the dirt-poor, but rather the beneficiaries of the PT government's social programmes. They have made real gains but want more, particularly much better public services, and are prepared to push hard for this. But, with the economy showing no signs of recovering buoyant rates of growth, it will be difficult for the government to respond to their demands without chipping away at the privileges of the elite, a sector that has not yet been harmed by the government's greater concern with social spending. It will be fascinating to see how this tension is resolved.

Transamazon Highway (Tony Morrison/South American Pictures)

# 7 The Amazon and the Environment

For those used to the Thames or the Potomac, the vastness of the Amazon River is hard to grasp. Rising in the Andes, flowing into the Atlantic, the 3,800-mile Amazon is the longest river in the world. Its statistics are mind-boggling.

The river basin, two-thirds of it in Brazil, drains an area as big as the United States (without Alaska). Seventeen of its tributaries are more than 1,000 miles long. Five hundred miles upriver from the sea, the Tapajós tributary is twelve miles wide. Marajó, the island that lies in the mouth of the Amazon, is about the size of Switzerland. Two thousand species of fish live in the Amazon basin, which covers one-twentieth of the world's land surface and contains one-sixth of its fresh water.

The rainforest proper covers 1.5 million square miles (145 million acres). Just one acre may contain up to 179 species of tree (the average for temperate forests is six). The Amazon rainforest contains the planet's largest gene reserve, its greatest store of biodiversity, a potential pharmaceutical cornucopia. Gold, uranium, bauxite, manganese, iron ore, cassiterite, oil, and gas have been found in the subsoil. The Amazon forest is bigger than the tropical forests in Africa, Asia, Central America and the rest of South America combined.

The Amazon basin is not just rainforest: it also contains savannah and mountains, including Brazil's highest mountain, the Pico da Neblina (2,994 m/9,823 ft). As deforestation advances around the fringes and follows the roads, there are now millions of acres of logged and cleared forest used for cattle pasture and farming, or just abandoned.

## *Myths and legends*

The Amazon has always been a source of myths and legends: lost explorers, cities of gold, fierce female warriors – dubbed Amazons by Spanish explorers after their namesakes in Greek mythology, which led to the river's name.

Home to giant snakes, electric fish and river dolphins, today the Amazon still attracts travellers and adventurers, as well as writers, TV travel journalists and celebrities. Archaeologists, anthropologists, biologists and botanists are still only scratching the surface of its vast unknown cultural and biological diversity, much of it already lost forever under new dams and roads. The forest's fantastic wealth has inspired equally fantastic plans to dominate and domesticate it, all of them eventually defeated by the conditions that have also earned it the title 'Green Hell'.

In the 1930s Henry Ford tried to tame the wild rubber tree into growing in neat lines in plantations: he planted three million trees at Fordlândia on the edge of the Tapajós river, only to see them wiped out by a fungus. In the 1960s, the Hudson Institute in the USA proposed damming the Amazon to turn it into a series of great lakes.

In 1967 American billionaire Daniel Ludwig bought four million acres of rainforest (at a cost of less than US$1 per acre) in

Passenger boats at an Amazon port (Julio Etchart)

the northern Amazon state of Amapá, with the idea of creating his own jungle empire. He cleared the forest and planted imported species such as the fast-growing gmelina from Asia, and California pine, to feed a pulp factory, which had been towed across the sea from Japan. He brought Dutch engineers to construct polders for rice paddies, and built a railway, hundreds of miles of roads, and a model company town with schools and a hospital. But many of the trees died, the rice did not flourish and malaria took its toll. A sprawling shanty town on stilts called Beiradão sprang up, home to 15,000 labourers and prostitutes. After spending an estimated US3 billion dollars on his project over 14 years, Ludwig gave up and pulled out. Brazilian companies took over the wood pulp factory, the only business to survive.

## Conquering the Amazon

The rainforest's impenetrability has always presented a challenge to outsiders, who, impatient with the slowness of river travel, have tried to drive railways or roads through it. When the rubber boom was at its peak towards the end of the 19th century, the British planned a railway to bring Bolivian rubber to Porto Velho where it would be shipped up river to Manaus. They gave up after disease, and attacks from indigenous groups and wild animals, took a huge toll.

In 1907 an American company took over, recruited 20,000 men from all over the world to work on the 200-mile rail track connecting the Mamoré and Madeira rivers, and completed it in 1912, just as the rubber boom was collapsing. Building the 'devil's railway' had cost the lives of more 6,000 workers, mostly from malaria, yellow fever and dysentery. In 1971 the railway was finally closed and the engines sold off as scrap.

The dream of conquering the Amazon remained. In 1972, 60 years after the ill-fated railway was opened, the Brazilian military decided it was time to link the Atlantic and Pacific Oceans by a 4,000-kilometre road, the Transamazonic Highway. At the time the north-east was in the grip of one of the periodic droughts that plague the region, leaving hundreds of thousands of landless rural families without food or water. The solution was to transport them to the Amazon, bringing 'the people without land', to what was dubbed 'the land without people', ignoring the existence of scores of indigenous tribes and riverside populations.

Installed in *agrovilas* – purpose-built settlements strung out along the new road – the new settlers were then forgotten, and left without assistance, transport or markets for their produce. At the time, hundreds of small farmers in the south were being expelled to make way for hydroelectric dams and the takeover of the land by giant soya farms. Some moved illegally over the border into Paraguay, where land was very cheap. Those who stayed began to demand land. The generals saw the state of Rondônia, in the western Amazon, as a useful safety valve for reducing the pressure for land reform.

In a modern equivalent of America's 19th-century wagon trails, hundreds of thousands of families were encouraged to travel 2,000 miles north and settle on the subsidized plots supplied by the government. Used to the temperate climate of the south, they found themselves in a hostile environment, lacking transport, battling malaria, tropical pests, torrential downfalls, and sometimes unfriendly indigenous populations. Many gave up and returned home, but, in the ten years between 1970 and 1980, Rondônia's population increased tenfold.

The military regime also offered tax incentives to big companies, multinational corporations, and banks to set up cattle ranches, which involved clearing millions of acres of virgin forest, and very often displacing traditional populations, among them rubber tappers. In the 1980s, Chico Mendes, a trade union organizer in the western state of Acre, led rubber tappers in collective actions known as *empates* to stop cattle ranchers felling the forest that provided them with their livelihoods. His success made him a marked man, and in December 1988 he was shot dead in his home by a cattle rancher's son. His murder made him an international 'eco-martyr', and the government felt obliged to implement his proposals for environmentally sustainable 'extractive reserves' for the rubber tappers and other forest collectors.

## Logging

Satellite pictures show that many indigenous reserves remain oases of untouched forest, surrounded by burnt and cleared land where cattle roam or soya is grown. Brazilians often claim that the Indians have too much land – the total area of all their reserves adds up to 11 per cent of the country's area, for a population of about 900,000. But this is to ignore the invaluable service provided by the reserves in protecting large areas of rainforest that would otherwise be cleared.

Elsewhere the region is coming under unprecedented assault. Using fraudulent documents, illegal loggers have been moving through the region in waves. First they extract the most valuable timber, including mahogany (until its export was banned in 2001), and then return for other hardwoods. In 2013 the landowners lobbied successfully to weaken the Forest Code, reducing protected areas along riversides and hilltops, and granting an amnesty to farmers who had cleared forest illegally.

## Minerals

The Amazon is rich in minerals – gold, iron ore, cassiterite, uranium. For thousands of poor Brazilians, the dream of Eldorado has lured them to brave the dangers and diseases of the forests and rivers in the hope of striking lucky. In the 1980s a big seam of gold was discovered near Marabá in the eastern Amazon, and thousands of wildcat panners, known in Brazil as *garimpeiros*, poured into the area, in one place digging out a huge hole with their bare hands, carrying sackfuls of earth hundreds of feet up rickety ladders to be panned for specks of gold. A makeshift town sprang up overnight around the hole, which became known as Serra Pelada (Bare Mountain). Very few became rich – most

Slashing and burning the forest (Julio Etchart)

spent their precious specks in the ramshackle bars and brothels that lined the dirt streets of the town, and many died in brawls and accidents. Thirty years later, Serra Pelada is being mined by machinery, but *garimpeiros* still invade indigenous reserves such as the Yanomami area in Roraima in the north, or work along the Tapajós river, diving from improvised rafts to hoover up sand and sediment from the riverbed and then filter it for gold.

In 1980 the military government launched another ambitious development project, Greater Carajás. Iron-ore deposits amounting to 18 billion tons had been discovered in the region near Marabá. 'Enough ore to pay off the foreign debt', said finance minister Antônio Delfim Neto. Needless to say, the foreign debt, which then stood at US$60 billion, continued to rise after the mine came on stream.

## Dams

The military began building big dams in the Amazon during the 1970s, but every government since has continued, and the current government of Dilma Rousseff is increasing the momentum, planning over 60 large dams in the region. The official justification is the need to meet the growing demand for energy from expanding cities and a growing population, but most of the energy will really go to energy-intensive mining projects, with a host of multinational companies planning to move in.

The giant dams may be cleaner than coal- or oil-fired plants, but they come at huge, irreparable cost to biodiversity, traditional populations and river life. Invaluable archaeological sites will be flooded, and much precious biodiversity will be lost. Belo Monte, already under construction on the River Xingu, will become the third-largest hydroelectric dam in the world. When it is completed, a stretch of the river used by the local indigenous communities will probably dry up for several months of the year, making it difficult for them to fish or travel. Norte Energia, the consortium building the dam, has distributed hundreds of plasma TVs and satellite dishes to the Indians – today's equivalent of the beads and mirrors handed out by earlier explorers – but many of the indigenous communities have not been bought off, and protests have dogged the construction work.

The government justifies the dam-building programme as a clean, renewable solution to Brazil's energy needs. But renewables like wind and solar are becoming cheaper, which is leading some people, including the prestigious Technological Institute of Aeronautics (ITA), to question the government's insistence on hydropower as the only solution.

## Environment

In 1972 the Brazilian delegation famously informed the Stockholm Environment Conference that development was more important than pollution. Twenty years later, Brazil hosted the 1992 Earth Summit, and was able to show off an array of specialized environmental agencies, from a special ministry down to state and municipal secretariats. Environmental prosecutors can now sue both state and private companies for crimes of pollution and contamination, while the 1988 constitution introduced the need for environmental impact studies before new development or industrial projects could go ahead.

The monitoring of the Amazon rainforest is now done in real time via satellite. But on the ground, inspectors are still needed to follow up when illegal deforestation is detected, and their number remains woefully inadequate. Even today, environmental concerns appear low in the government's agenda, and the authorities set a bad example by reducing the area of some national conservation areas to make way for dams.

One of the biggest threats to the preservation of the rainforest comes from large landowners and agribusiness companies, particularly exporters of soya and meat, who have formed a powerful lobby represented by an all-party bloc – the *bancada ruralista* – in Congress, with an estimated 200 members. Having successfully weakened the Forest Code, they began a new campaign in 2013 to gain control over the demarcation of indigenous lands. Without a majority in congress, the PT governments have allowed this bloc to set the environmental agenda in exchange for their votes on other bills.

By 2014, almost one-fifth of the Amazon rainforest had been cleared. Another important biomass – the Atlantic forest, which once covered the entire coastline of Brazil – has been reduced to only 8 per cent of its original size. Each year farmers are clearing 8 million acres of the Cerrado, the vast savannah in central Brazil where many of the Amazon tributaries rise, to plant crops and pasture.

In the early 2000s the environment ministry, under Marina Silva, created huge conservation areas in the Amazon region and dozens of extractive and sustainable reserves for existing populations. But it is the agriculture and mining ministries who hold political power in the government, and they tend to see the forest as an obstacle to progress, an unproductive area that must be conquered and put to work for urban Brazil, providing energy and export earnings. This short-sighted attitude means that the future of the rainforest is at risk.

### Climate change

In 2013 the Brazilian Panel on Climate Change, a member of the UN's international panel, the IPCC, produced a report showing that climate change caused by global warming will drastically affect Brazil's rainfall, and consequently its agriculture. The 345 scientists who make up the Brazilian Panel predicted that, if the present upward trends in greenhouse gas emissions continue, average temperatures in Brazil will be 3–6°C higher in 2100 compared with their level at the end of the 20th century. Tornados, once rare but already becoming more frequent, will become a regular occurrence.

While rainfall in the Amazon region could fall by 40 per cent, affecting the supply of water to reservoirs, reducing energy production and damaging biodiversity, it is expected to increase in the south and south-east of the country, increasing flooding and mudslides, which are already common events.

### Air pollution

In the big cities like Rio and São Paulo, car ownership has been encouraged, and local governments have invested heavily in road improvements while neglecting public transport. A study showed that 4,656 people died as a result of air pollution in São Paulo in 2011, three times the number killed in traffic accidents. The outlawing in 2014 of dirty petrol marks a step in the right direction.

The example of Curitiba, capital of Paraná state, which successfully bucked the trend and gave priority to articulated buses run along special bus-lanes was not followed in other capitals. In 2013, however, the authorities were shaken by huge popular protests demanding better, cheaper transport. As a result, the newly elected mayor of São Paulo, the PT's Fernando Haddad, began to create hundreds of miles of bus-lanes, squeezing those for cars. Now buses travel faster than cars. This followed years of apathy by previous administrators, and an inexplicable failure to extend São Paulo's metro system, which was begun in 1969, and carries four million passengers a day, but still has only 64 stations. Run by the state government, it has been dogged by allegations of bribery and corruption.

Another major environmental concern is the state of many of Brazil's rivers, especially those that flow through cities. São Paulo's River Tietê, once the scene of rowing regattas, is now little more than an open sewer, fed by hundreds of factories upstream. Rio's beautiful, mountain-ringed Guanabara Bay is also heavily polluted with oil and detritus from tankers and ships, as well as urban waste. Internationally financed projects to clean up the waters are now under way.

One thing Brazil has excelled at is the recycling of soft-drink cans, and this is because it is an income earner for the poor. *Catadores*, as the rubbish collectors are called, earn modest incomes by piling their handcarts high with the paper and cardboard left on pavements by shops and offices and selling it to the municipal authorities. The important role of the *catadores*, most of them now grouped in co-operatives, is increasingly recognized, but large-scale recycling lags behind that found in other countries.

Recyling cans is a way of life for some poor people (Sue Cunningham)

# Where to Go, What to See, What to Do

Wherever you go in Brazil, the language is Portuguese and the passion is football, but each region has a very distinctive flavour. The distances are huge, so unless you are ready to face several days on a bus, flying makes sense. Brazil is no longer a cheap country, but by booking ahead you can get good deals.

### Rail travel

Trains are rare, run-down, and slow. The exceptions are the breathtakingly beautiful line that runs past waterfalls and across gorges from Curitiba down to the port of Paranaguá on the Paraná coast. Or in the north, the thrice-weekly sixteen-hour trip that takes you 550 miles south-west from São Luis to the iron-ore mine at Carajás in the eastern Amazon. Unbelievably, there is no longer a passenger train between Rio and São Paulo.

### Buses

Hitchhiking is not advised, but buses are plentiful, although no longer very cheap. Half of Brazil always seems to be travelling; buses and bus terminals are always crowded. If you can afford it, it is worth getting the ônibus leito (literally, bed-bus), which offers you a fully reclining seat and unlimited coffee and mineral water as it rolls through the countryside, night or day.

### Rio de Janeiro

The statue of Christ which overlooks the city of Rio de Janeiro with outstretched arms has been voted one of the seven wonders of the modern world, and it is not hard to see why. On moonlit nights the floodlit statue shines over the city below. When it is overcast, the statue drifts in and out of the clouds. From the mountain on which the statue is built there is a breathtaking view of Rio below, squeezed between the mountains and the sea. During the day, hang gliders float down from the Gávea peak. The mountains are sharp and dramatic; geologically they are still young, and so age has not yet smoothed and rounded them.

The famous beaches of Copacabana and Ipanema are lined with elaborate kiosks serving seafood and fresh coconut juice, to be drunk from the big green nuts through a straw. The wide pavement which runs the full length of the beaches is full of joggers, walkers, and just amblers of all ages, dressed in every sort of gear. Cyclists speed or pedal slowly along the bike track.

In the morning the beaches are crowded with sunbathers, but later on the sand becomes a vast sports arena, with people playing football, volleyball, and variations of both. At night pop and rock concerts draw audiences of hundreds of thousands. Sundays often see religious rallies on the beach – even the Pope set up his altar on Copacabana beach and preached to a multitude of the rain-soaked faithful during his visit in 2013.

Many Rio streets are lined with trees, offering welcome shade. Fruit sellers and popcorn vendors set up shop at the corners. Magnificent tall imperial palms can be found in the Flamengo area and in the Botanical Gardens. Here and there you come across small parks full of children playing around statues of historical figures – even Baden Powell has a bust, although the man honoured is the founder of scouting, not the musician.

Downtown, Flamengo Park curves along beside the sea, full of volleyball, basketball, and soccer pitches. The historic Glória church is perched on a hillside behind the park, reached by a steep funicular railway. From the church there is a magnificent view of the Bay of Guanabara and Sugar Loaf mountain, reached by cable cars. Planes take off and land at nearby Santos Dumont airport, where the runways are bounded on three sides by the sea. The airport is named after the man who, for Brazilians, is the father of aviation, having made a flight in a fixed-wing heavier-than-air machine in 1906. A colourful mural of the aviation pioneer surrounded by flying machines covers an entire inside wall of the airport, used for domestic flights only.

The quickest way to get around in Rio is on the Metro – it is basic but efficient, with the occasional snatch of bossa nova music between announcements to remind you where you are. The network is small – only 35 stations, with more under construction – but it will take you quickly to and from Copacabana and the downtown area.

Taking the bus is not for the faint-hearted – passengers need to be fairly acrobatic even to board the bus with its high step, and quick on their feet as drivers alternate between dawdling in traffic jams and speeding along open stretches, taking corners fast, jerking to a halt at bus stops, crashing gears, and all the while carrying on a conversation with the conductor.

The city is called Rio de Janeiro because the Portuguese explorers who discovered its natural harbour on 1 January 1565 thought at first it was a river. It lies on the edge of Guanabara Bay, ringed by mountains. Hundreds of cargo ships lie at anchor in the bay – a reminder that Rio is very much a port city. In the summer, six or seven cruise ships a day line up in the dock area, disgorging thousands of passengers.

The dock area is enjoying a makeover – an ugly road viaduct flyover has been demolished, and the warehouses are being transformed into cultural centres. At the moment many are used during carnival to build and store the gigantic floats.

Over six million people live in Rio (they are called *cariocas*), many in apartment blocks crammed higgedly-piggedly below mountainside shanty towns. Most of the *favelas* in the centre have been 'pacified' – cleared of the drug gangs that ran them – and provided with the basic utility services they previously lacked, including community-friendly police. The drug bosses have moved their operations to more distant *favelas*.

The main Olympic site is located to the west of Copacabana, beyond Rio's fastest-developing suburb, the Barra da Tijuca, a long beach now lined by wealthy condominiums. Events will also take place at three other locations – the Maracanã football stadium, the Lagoa (lagoon) and Deodoro. Thanks to the huge 2013 demonstrations against corruption and public waste, the perfectly good pool, school and indigenous museum next to Maracanã were saved from being torn down to make way for parking and a shopping centre.

The dark side of Rio – violence, drug traffickers, militias, trigger-happy police who shoot first and ask questions later – is always there. A famous Brazilian historian, Sérgio Buarque de Holanda, invented the concept of the 'cordial' Brazilian, which is hard to square with the high level of violence. What he really meant was that, in Brazilians, emotion takes precedence over reason, including violent emotion. So do not expect rationality in Rio.

Expect emotion, good and bad. On the whole, you will find *cariocas* welcoming, friendly and always ready for a joke.

## São Paulo

The largest city in the Americas, São Paulo pulsates with life. Traffic is terrible, with hundreds of kilometres of traffic jams on the worst days. A million motorbikes weave in and out of the nose-to-tail cars.

Wherever you look, growing forests of smart new residential towers, 20 or 30 floors high, sprout above districts of single-storey housing. At night the metropolis throbs with music of every style, while thousands of restaurants and bars cater to every possible taste and pocket. Without the natural beauty of Rio, São Paulo offers a variety of museums, including a football museum, a handful of historic buildings which have survived since the city's foundation in 1554, some beautiful old railway stations and markets, colourful noisy street markets and lots of culture, including graffiti. The Metro, already too crowded for comfort, offers works of art and book-vending machines in some stations, and will take you all the way out to the World Cup stadium Itaquerão, located in a working-class suburb in the city's culturally bleak east side.

## Salvador

Brazil's capital when the slave trade was at its height, it still has the highest proportion of black people in the country. Syncretism has produced a unique mix of Catholic and African *candomblé* religions. Musical creativity is at its height in Salvador, with the powerful drumbeat of Olodum and other mass percussion bands echoing round the cobbled streets, and the annual invention of new Carnival rhythms blaring out to the massed crowds that dance behind the *trios elétricos* (mobile band platforms) and the gentle twang of the *berimbau* players. South or north of Salvador is lotus-eater's paradise – soft sandy beaches where you can lie under palm trees sipping from a fresh coconut and snacking on freshly caught seafood. Brazil's Atlantic coast offers hundreds of beaches, some commercialized, many unspoilt.

## Manaus

A thousand miles upriver from the Atlantic is the Amazon capital, where the few reminders of the rubber boom include the beautiful 19th-century opera house, and the floating dock built to accommodate an annual rise and fall of 50 feet. The city itself is nondescript, badly planned and polluted. The main interest remains the river, with the nearby encounter of the dark waters of the Rio Negro and the muddy waters of the Rio Solimões, which meet to form the Amazon. There is now a bridge connecting Manaus to the other side of the Negro river, but the road south is unpaved and precarious. The main highway into the depths of the Amazon forest remains the river, with boats of all sizes carrying cargo and passengers.

## Belo Horizonte

Inaugurated as Minas Gerais's new capital at the end of the 19th century, Belo Horizonte ('beautiful horizon' in English) was named for its views of nearby mountains. It was the second of Brazil's planned cities, and, while it has long since sprawled well beyond its original limits, it retains some of the old charm. The metropolitan area is now Brazil's third-largest, after São Paulo and Rio, though the city has a slightly more traditional feel in comparison. Nevertheless, there is plenty to do here, from catching a show at the Palácio das Artes, to visiting the Central Market to taste the region's famous local cheese and to sample *cachaça*, a popular Brazilian spirit made from sugar cane, much of which is produced locally in Minas Gerais.

Drinkers will find themselves at home here. A local saying runs 'Belo Horizonte não tem mar, então vamos pro bar!' ('There's no sea in Belo Horizonte, so let's go to the bar!'), and the city has become known as Brazil's bar capital. Moreover, in Parque das Mangabeiras, the city boasts one of the largest urban parks in Latin America. Situated on the mountainside at the southern edge of the city, the park offers good opportunities for walking and some spectacular views, while for the less adventurous there are squares in which to find rest, food and drinks stalls, and even a bus service to save you sweating up the trails.

Belo Horizonte also makes a good base from which to explore the many points of interest in Minas Gerais, including the nearby Serra do Curral; old colonial towns such as Ouro Preto, Tiradentes and Diamantina; and the unmissable Inhotim, a vast, beautiful, open-air art museum and gardens located south-west of the city.

## Amazon

To get a feeling of the real width of the mighty Amazon, travel to Santarém, where the huge Tapajós tributary flows into it. Buy a hammock and two lengths of rope and go down to the quayside where the riverboats wait for the evening tide to sail to Oriximiná or Óbidos. Join the other passengers in the forest of gently swaying hammocks; fall asleep to the throbbing of the engine as the boat chugs across the river, with the moon shining on the water. Wake at dawn and discover you have exchanged the open sea of the Amazon for the confines of a river. A slug of coffee from the communal thermos flask, a quick wash, and you can stand at the rail and watch life on the riverbank, children splashing and swimming, women washing clothes, men silently paddling canoes.

## Ouro Preto

Eight hours from Rio, ten hours from São Paulo, Ouro Preto, recognized by UNESCO as the most complete 18th-century colonial town in the world, is a tightly packed mass of cobbled streets, houses, and richly decorated churches, built with the gold of the local mines. Look for Aleijadinho's work, scattered in different places. Semi-precious stones and soapstone artefacts are on sale everywhere.

## Tips for travellers

### PEOPLE

Brazilians respond much better to a smile than a shout, to a joke rather than an insult. Don't be afraid of physical contact: Brazilians, like other Latins, do not have the same horror of touching each other that most Anglo-Saxons have. Everyone shakes hands all the time, friends and often mere acquaintances kiss once, twice, or even three times on the cheek, men pat or thump each other on the back. When they are talking to each other, Brazilians not only wave their hands around but feel the need to touch the person they are talking to.

## SAFETY

Brazil has a well-deserved reputation for petty crime, especially in the big cities like Rio, São Paulo, and Recife, where muggers and bag-snatchers are common, and sometimes gangs of thieves raid restaurants or beaches. However, you can reduce the risks by taking a few basic precautions.

Be streetwise – leave passports, credit cards and large amounts of money in the hotel safe, and carry only small amounts of cash when you go out. Take your camera in an ordinary plastic bag, not around your neck. Don't wear expensive jewellery or watches. In Rio and other seaside resorts, take as little as possible to the beach. Even clothes can get stolen while you are swimming! Don't walk on Rio's Copacabana beach at night – it's a notorious mugging spot. Don't attempt to visit shanty towns unless you are accompanied by guides or somebody who knows the residents.

## HEALTH

Taking a few precautions can also avert health problems which might otherwise spoil your trip. Don't drink tap water – mineral water is generally available. Don't eat unwashed salad or fruit – market gardeners use liberal amounts of pesticide. And don't overdo the sunbathing, especially around midday. Fifteen minutes is the maximum without protection.

You have to worry about malaria only if you are going away from the main tourist centres into certain areas of the Amazon. It is more prevalent during the rainy season, which runs from October to April. Mosquito-nets can be purchased at any Amazon town.

If you pick up a bug or parasite, go to an English-speaking Brazilian doctor, because he will be more familiar with the symptoms.

Pharmacies sell many medicines over the counter that would be available only on prescription in UK and the US. Tampons and condoms are sold everywhere in pharmacies and supermarkets.

## WOMEN TRAVELLERS

Women increasingly travel on their own. Except in the more remote places, lone women should not encounter any problems.

## CHANGING MONEY

Changing money has become much easier: you can do it at banks, travel agencies, and exchange (*cambio*) shops. Hotels also change money, but give a lower rate. Outside the main cities, changing money can be more difficult, and international credit cards are not always accepted, so it is best to change sufficient before you travel to the interior.

## SOUVENIRS

The best places to buy souvenirs are in the open-air markets. Never accept the first price, always haggle. The government's Indian affairs agency, FUNAI, runs shops at the major airports which offer indigenous artefacts at reasonable prices.

**São Paulo:** Praça da República and Praça da Liberdade (oriental fair). Markets are held on Saturdays and Sundays.

**Rio:** Praça General Osório (Ipanema) and along the beaches: São Cristovão market (Zona Norte).

**Belém:** Ver o Peso market, renowned for charms and virility potions of all sorts.

**Belo Horizonte:** The 'Hippie Fair' on Sundays, located on the Avenida Afonso Pena, is deservedly famous. The Central Market is also a favourite spot, selling countless arts and crafts products.

## CHILDREN

Because of baby-trafficking and paedophile scandals, foreigners taking small children or babies out of Brazil may be required to prove their relationship with them, so if travelling with children, take their birth certificates with you.

## DRUGS

Brazilian prisons are crowded with foreigners caught attempting to smuggle drugs, usually cocaine or marijuana. Brazil is a major corridor for cocaine produced in Bolivia, Colombia, and Peru. The police are very alert, sentences are long, and prison conditions are harsh.

## FOOD AND DRINK

Every region of Brazil has its specialities, its own dishes. On the coast, seafood and fish dishes predominate. In cattle-rearing states, it's all about meat. In São Paulo, thanks to the huge immigrant population, you can eat excellent Japanese, Italian, Arab, German or Spanish food. There are even (expensive) English and Irish pubs, where fish and chips are on offer.

### Drinks

*Caipirinha* = delicious cocktail of sugarcane rum, limes, sugar and ice

*Caipiroska* = *caipirinha* with vodka instead of rum

*Choppe* = draught beer

*Cerveja* = Beer (Brazilian beer is more like lager, always drunk chilled, or *estúpidamente gelado* – stupidly cold)

*Suco* = fruit juice (choose bars with fresh fruit hanging above the counter, otherwise your juice might be made from pulp)

*Caldo de cana* = sugarcane juice, can be served with lemon, ginger

*Agua de coco* = coconut water, best drunk cold

*Cafezinho* = small black coffee – beware, in non-tourist bars, it often comes already loaded with sugar.

*Vinho* = wine: Brazil produces some good wine but Chilean and Argentine wines are cheaper and usually, better.

### Meals

*Feijoada* = black bean stew served with pork trotters, rice, manioc flour, kale and slices of orange. Once slave food, now a national institution, traditionally served on Wednesdays and Saturdays

*Muqueca* = seafood stew with coconut milk

*Churrasco* = barbecue – cuts of different meats served on spits at the table

### Snacks

*Coxinha* = chicken and mashed potato covered in breadcrumbs

*Pastel* = pasty, fried in deep oil on the spot, containing cheese, meat or other ingredients

### Kilo restaurants

Buffets of hot and cold food, you pay by weight.